James Safo
Microsoft specialist, Cissco computer technician
Dip. Computer, LLM (Master of Laws o/g) BA (Hons)

QUIK REFERENCE

Preface

This publication covers data for both beginners and advance levels of Microsoft, word, power Point, Excel and Access. The protection against computers' attack, and the parts and functions of the operating system and the internet. In addition there are 310 question to test your knowledge and follow by answers to these questions.

Computer is electronic device intended to accept data, perform prescribed precise and logical operations at high speed, and display the results of these operations. Types of computers include Mainframes, desktop and laptop, tablets, and smartphones. It consist of hard and soft drive. Computer come in different forms, analogy and digital or Hybrid. Micro: Computer characteristic include clone, electronic brain, calculator, artificial intelligence, data processor, number cruncher. Analog computer, devices in which continuously variable physical quantities. Digital computer operates with numbers expressed directly as digits. Hybrid a computer system consisting of a combination of analog and digital.

Dedicate

I dedicate this 0ver 410 pages book
"Computing for Beginners" to two good friends.

Faustina Aspee Adu

and

Theresa Gyamea

Acknowledgement

I give credit to Almighty God for given me the
knowledge and guidance to write this book

About the Author

Qualifications include master's degree in Laws, BA(Hons) in law and accounts, lecturer Cert Ed, qualified general and psychiatry nurse, counselling and a lot more as listed at the end of this publication.

Have solely written and published over 40 titles books on all major religious faiths in the world, books on academic: Law, accounts, criminology, counselling, business (4 books), psychology, health, over 700 Poems in (5 books), History Counselling, Psychology, sweet and Sour women, Women are superior to men etc.

Some of the religion books have been translated from English into Arabic, chines, French and Spanish.

Please check the end of this publication for my extraordinary qualifications and published books were given to me by God inspiration as living memory of God's prophets.

Content   Approx. Page

Synopsis
processing program launch
selecting a preferred template
Choose your preferred design.
inserting pictures
changing the document layout
Inserting margins
Changing the orientation
Adding or removing columns
Changing indention and spacing
using the review tab
Choosing the page size
setting header or footer
Redo and undo
using the file tab
Saving the document
shutting down the computer

Adding quick styles
Change style
Apply selected style
Creating the table of content
select the number of levels of headings
Updating the table of content
To update the page numbers only,
Deleting the table of contents
Setting water marks
Setting custom watermark
set a picture as watermark
To remove the watermark
Mailing documents
Translator document
Page Orientation
Set Page Margins
Set Header 0r Footer
Text Alignment
Font choices
Font size
Font: **(B I U)**
Create a folder to put your file into
Move folder to Address Bar
Navigate to Word application document
Font colour
Insert Table
Line spacing: Increase/Decrease
Heading HI /H2
Columns
Insert Pictures
Spell-check
Find and replace
New document
Save regularly
Shut computer down OR log Off

of emergencies Procedure

Hard disk. Partition. Active partition.
Primary partition. Extended Partition
Cylinder. File allocation or cluster
Drive Mapping

MSCONFIG:
SYSTEM. INI and WIN.INI.files
REFEDIT. REGEDT32
MODES. Safe mode
Safe mode with network

Chapter   1

About the Mouse

Use your finger to click right or left mouse
Left Mouse   Right mouse

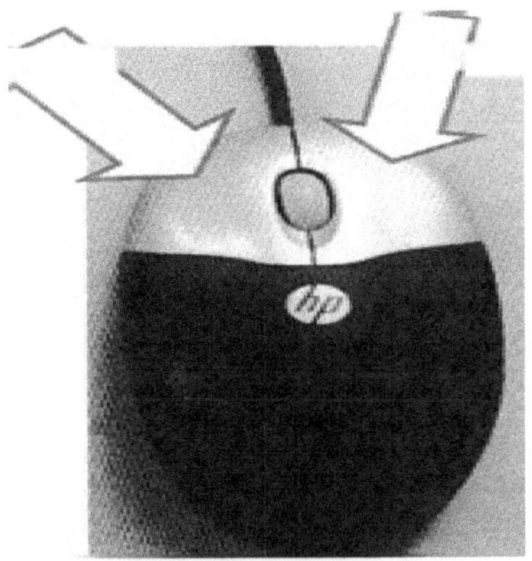

Start Computer

First Press Power Button on box or laptop

Second Wait for password user name screen

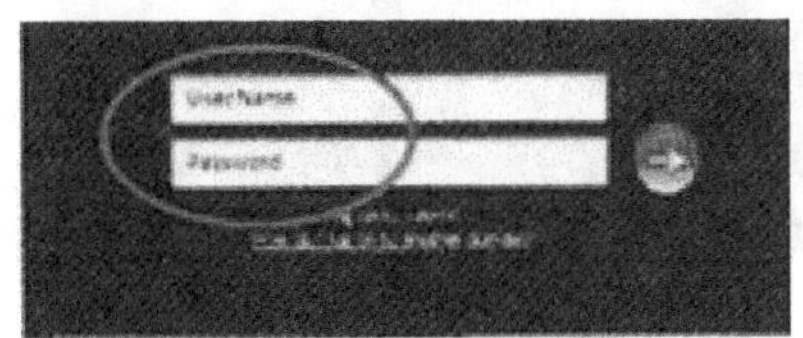

User name and password

Type your User name and password into the text boxes and press enter

User Name:

 Password:

Note: Don't leave any character spaces in between Example

You now see your Desktop Screen

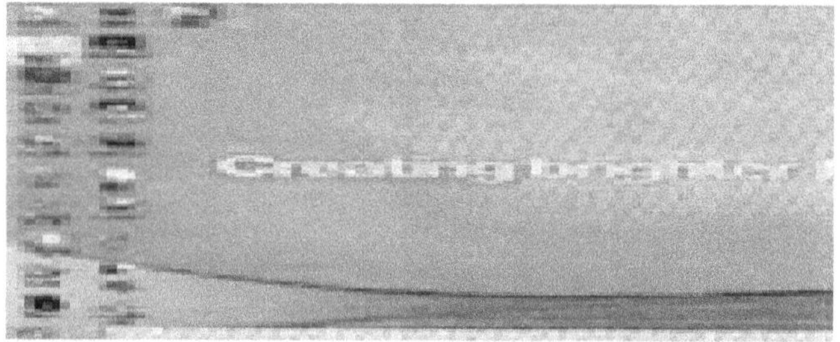

Word scree is set as default

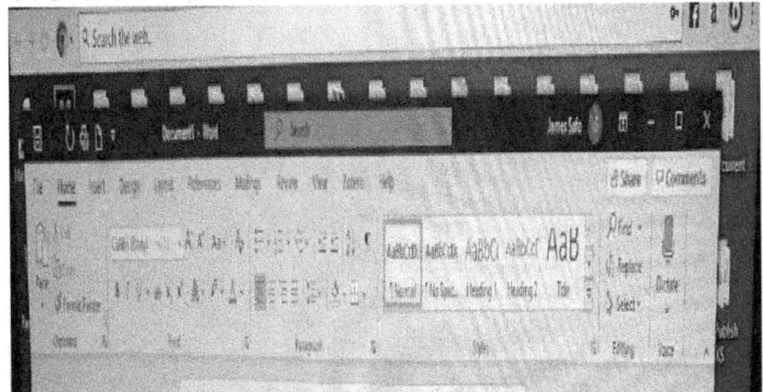

Enhanced Word Ribbon

Bottom screen of word

The Ribbon contains all the controls you need

Tabs: Reveals icons you need to use

Icons: All the images on the ribbon used for formatting

Groups :"Category of formatting tools grouped together

Tabs: Click on a tab to find the formatting tools you need This is on Home tab with tools to format text

Example

Font drop-down arrow reveals Font Dialogue Box

Chapter 2

Keyboard

Keyboard of computer

KEYBOARD COMMANDS

CONTROL+A=Select all

CONTROL+B=Apply bold

CONTROL+C=Copy

CONTROL+D=Font Changes

CONTROL+*E=Centre Align*

CONTROL+F=Find

CONTROL+G=Go To

CONTROL+H=Replace

CONTROL+I Italics

CONTROL+JFully Justified

CONTROL+K=Insert Hyperlink

CONTROL+L=Left Align

CONTROL+M=Increase Indent

CONTROL+N=New Blank Document

CONTROL+O=Open Document

CONTROL+P=Print Document

CONTROL+R=Right Align

CONTROL+S=Save Document

CONTROL+T=Sets 2nd line indent

CONTROL+U=Underline

CONTROL+V = Paste

CONTROL+W=Close Document

CONTROL+X=Cut

CONTROL+Y =Redo

CONTROL+Z=Undo

CONTROL 1= Single Line Spacing +

 CONTROL 2= Double Line Spacing +

CONTROL 5 =1.5 Line Spacing

F1=Help

F7=Spell check

F12= Save As

Word (Microsoft) for Beginners

Synopsis

Microsoft invented a useful processing program known as Microsoft office. Using this processing program, one can format text and type it when a graphic setting resembles page paper. The processing program also has extra features that include images, tables, and advanced texting features, allowing the user to customize the document further that one is working on. With advancements in technology, various additions and updates have been employed to make this program better and useful. As a result, of personal computers and Macs, it is a widely used process with billions of people using it to perform various functions worldwide. In many office jobs, knowing utilizing this program is advantageous since it is used in many offices. As a result, many schools teach the basics in this program to enable students to have a general knowledge of the program. In offices, it can be used to edit business documents like reports, emails, and letters. For a beginner, this guide gives the essential functions of the Microsoft word program and its uses.

The first thing before starting the program is creating the computer and then typing the computer's password.

Step 1:

Microsoft word processing program launch

I)   Click on the start key, then search Microsoft word as shown in fig 1a

II)   Click on open for the program to launch as shown below in fig.1b

Apart from typing the documents, there is various mouse navigation important to a word document user. Double-clicking the mouse selects a word while triple-clicking selects the paragraph. Clicking and dragging the mouse selects a text from the first click was up to where the mouse is released. Additionally, right-clicking a mouse opens a pop-up menu, which changes depending on where clicked, while left-clicking selects objects.

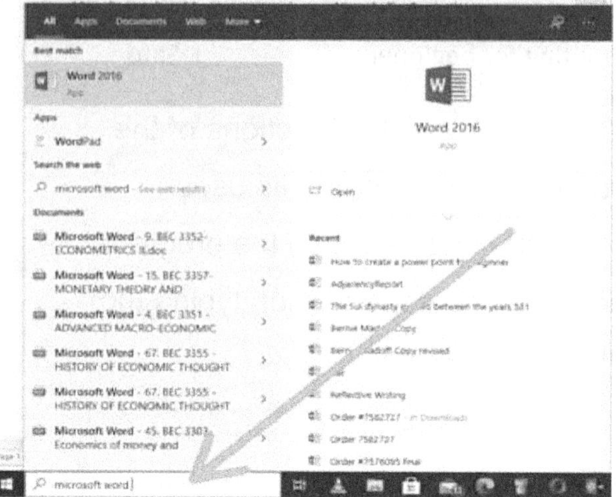

Fig. 1a

After typing the word Microsoft word, the program name will appear on the desktop.

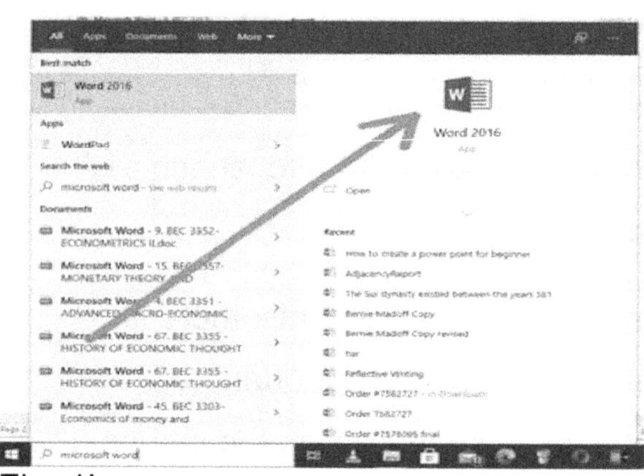

Fig. 1b

The next thing to do for the program to launch is clicking on open.

Step: 2

selecting a preferred template

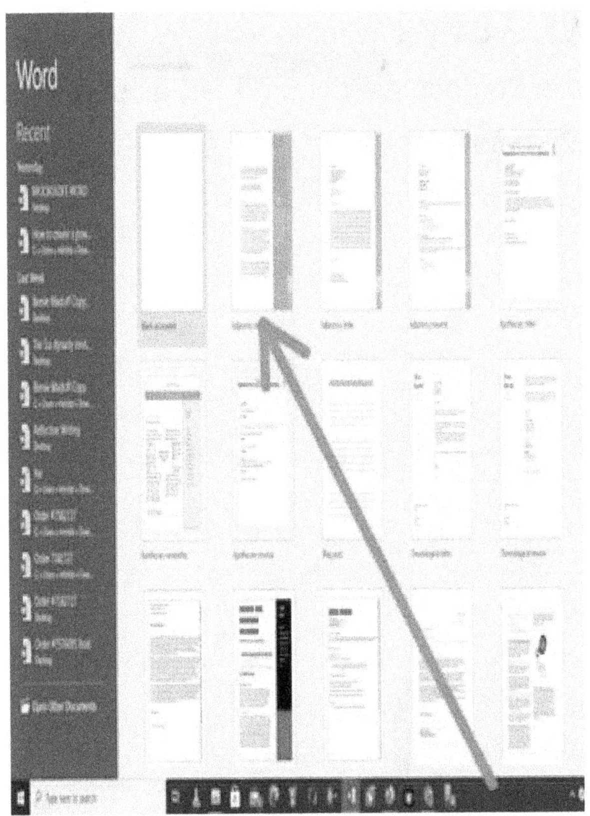

Fig 2a.

When the program launch on your computer, it will bring on the screen windows 0ption of choosing the desired template. If you want to start a new document, you will select the blank document template. On the left side of the screen, the three will appear recently save documents, and if you want to read any, you will click on the old document you prefer, as shown in figure 2b below.

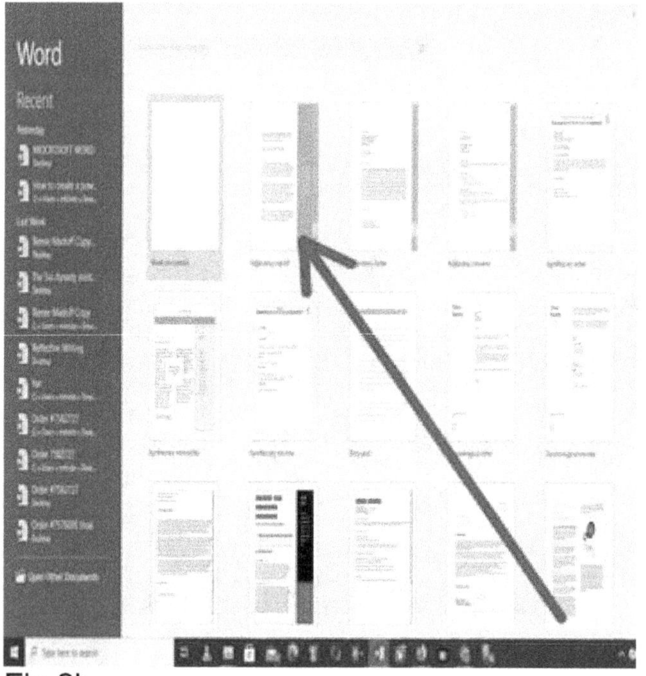

Fig 2b.

Step 3:

Choose your preferred design.

After the MS word has fully launched, you will be required to choose your appropriate design for the document. To get the preferred method, you will click on the design the appears on the ribbon- a ribbon shows various tabs that consist of the file, home, insert, design, layout, reference, mailings, review, and view. After clicking on the Design tab, it is always good to explore all the designs that appear on the screen, and by this, you will get one that will be appealing to you. As much as the designs may look almost the same, you preview before making it the chosen method. When you select a plan that you prefer, it will automatically be made the default design for the entire word document for that particular time. However, the word document can have different designs; while writing, you can select the part you want to change the design for and choose your preferred design for that particular part. After you have selected your design, it's now time that you can start typing in your document.

Fig 3.

Step 4:

inserting pictures

If you want to add pictures, graphs, and charts, you will need to follow the following ways to insert them. Click the Insert tab, and in this, you will find multiple options where you can choose exactly what you want to insert. You will find the tabs to add pictures, tables, add symbols, add shapes, and other various diagrams. In your text, you move your cursor in free space and then click on the insert and then select the add picture. The pop-up message will request you to choose the image your need from the personal computer. If it's tables that you want to insert, you will see options to draw your tables or choose from the existing tables after clicking on the insert. If you need to insert shapes and graphs, you will click on the insert and select the maps you need, whether bar graphs, pie charts, line graphs, etc.

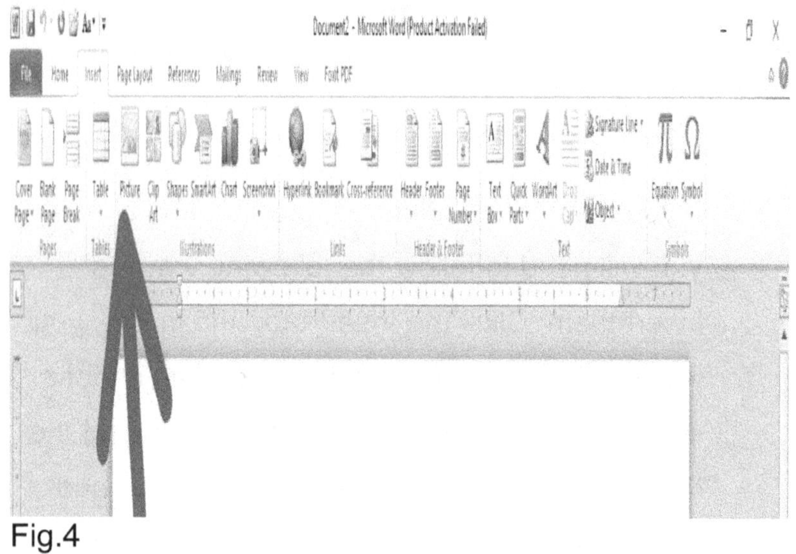

Fig.4

Step 5:

changing the document layout

The layout tab enables the user to set the document in the preferred layout. This is done by adjusting the document's margins for the paper's section or the whole form. Also, changing the page orientation from portrait to landscape or from landscape to portrait is possible. The user can also choose the size of the page and can also add or remove columns. In this tab,

changing the indention and spacing of the document in the paragraph section is possible.

i)   Inserting margins

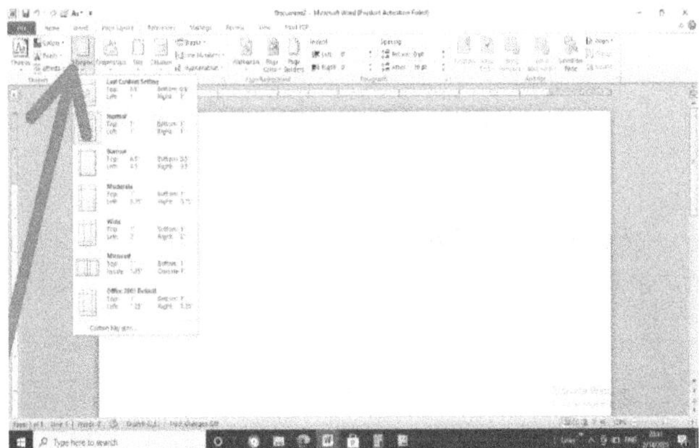

Fig.5a

ii)   Changing the orientation

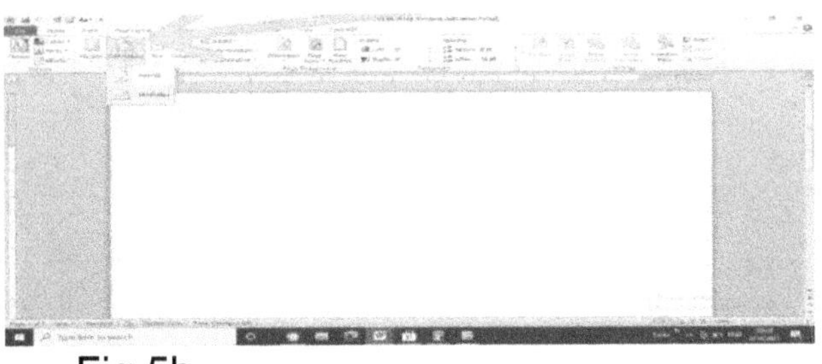

Fig.5b

iii) Choosing the page size

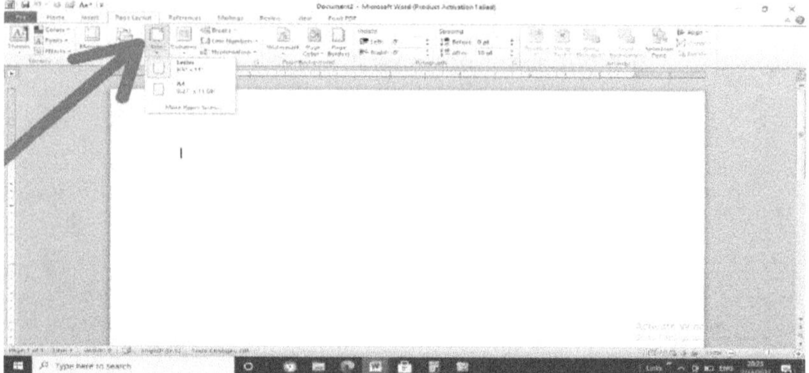

Fig.5c

iv)   Adding or removing columns

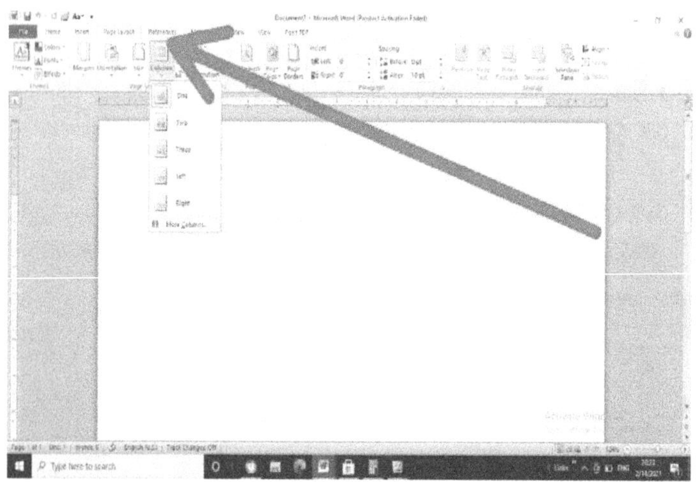

Fig.5d

vi)   Changing indention and spacing

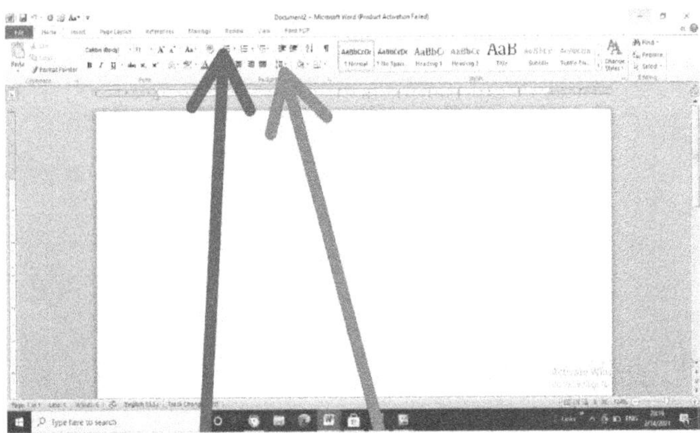

Fig. 5e

Step 6:

using the review tab

The tab has various functions such as proofing, language, accessibility changes, and speech functions. Additionally, the grammar and spelling function is also in this tab and is essential since the user can check any grammar and spelling errors.

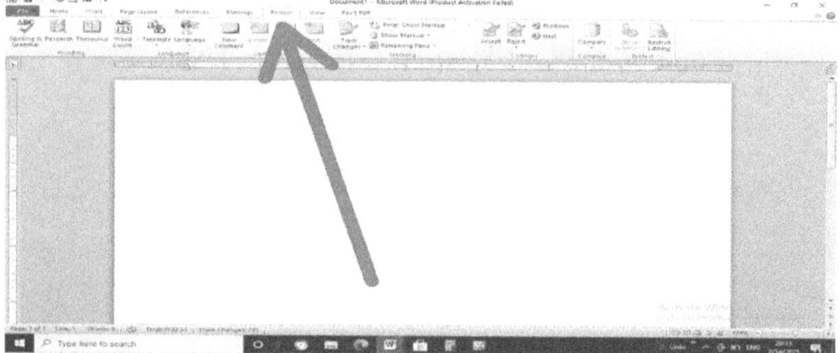

Fig. 6

Step 7:
setting header or footer

To insert header and footer, click on insert to add the preferred header or footer.

Redo and undo

a typed is also possible and deleted text to come back to the document. Undo and redo are done by pressing the undo tab or the redo tab. The green arrow illustrates the undo tab, while the red one is a redo tab

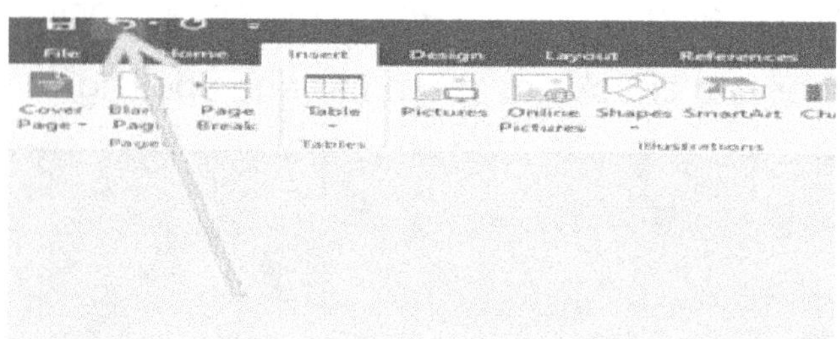

Fig.7b

Step 8:

Using the file tab

The file tab is used when through with the document. This tab is where saving, printing, sharing the document, and publishing the document are done. After finishing with the document, it is essential to save the document before proceeding to other steps to choose the record's preferred location. Saving the document enables one to find the document for future reference or after the document is accidentally closed without finishing the intended purpose.

Saving the document

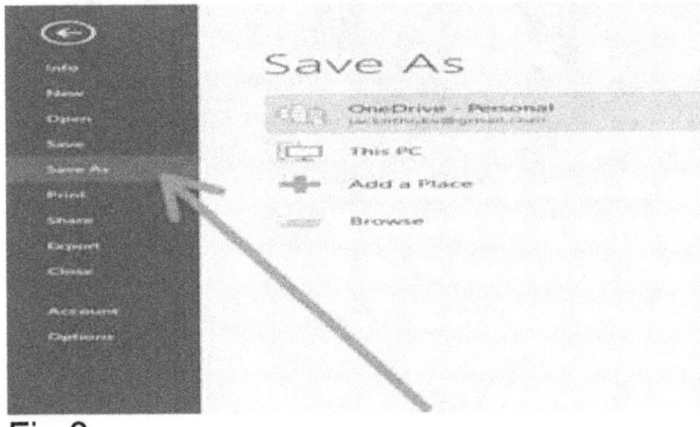

Fig.8

Step 9:

 shutting down the computer

After finishing using Microsoft word, you close
the program then shut down the computer.
Shutting down is done by clicking on the start
menu, then click on power, and finally clicking on
shutdown for the computer to shut down.

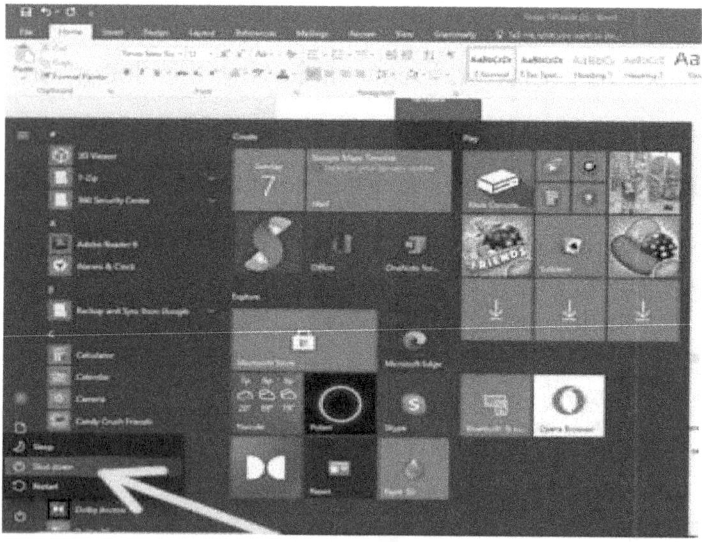

Fig. 9

Chapter 4

Word (Microsoft) Advance)

a. Adding quick styles

The steps to follow to add quick styles on the selected text include:

i. Select the text you wish to add the style. Using the style, you can change the selected text to be the heading or subheading of your document.

ii. Click the home tab move the mouse pointer to style gallery, the selected portion of the text will change its style. For more styles click more styles tab. See fig. 1 below

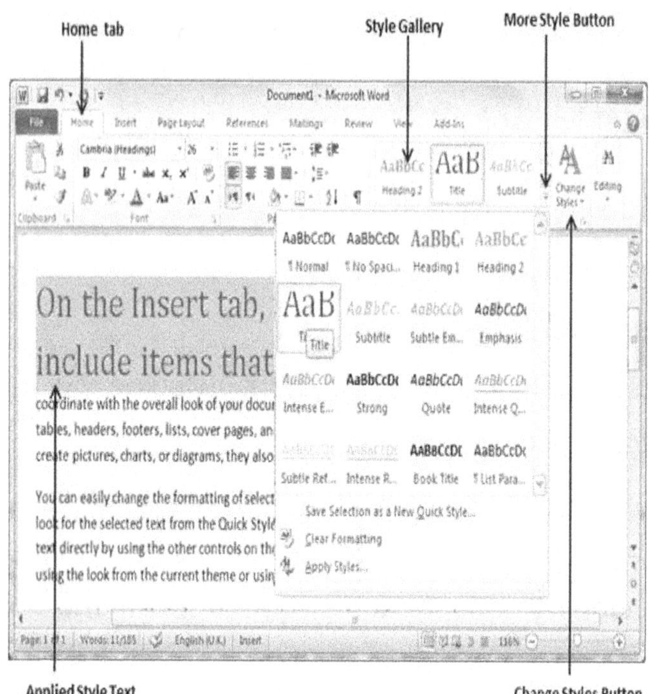

Fig. 1

. To apply the style, click over the style (with the text still selected). You will find that the style has been changed. See fig. 2 below

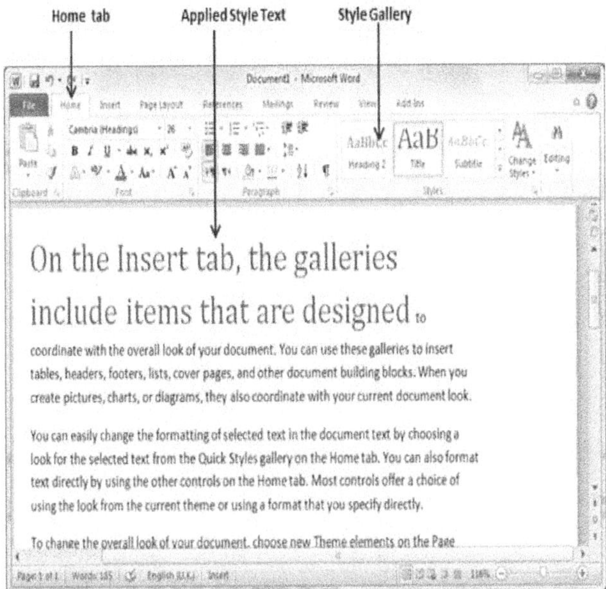

Fig 2

iv.   To bring the text to its normal appearance, click the normal tab

Change styles.

Allow you to change the default font, color, paragraph, spacing and style of the document.

To change the style:

i.   Open the document, click the home tab then change style button; all the possible styles are displayed. See fig. 3 below

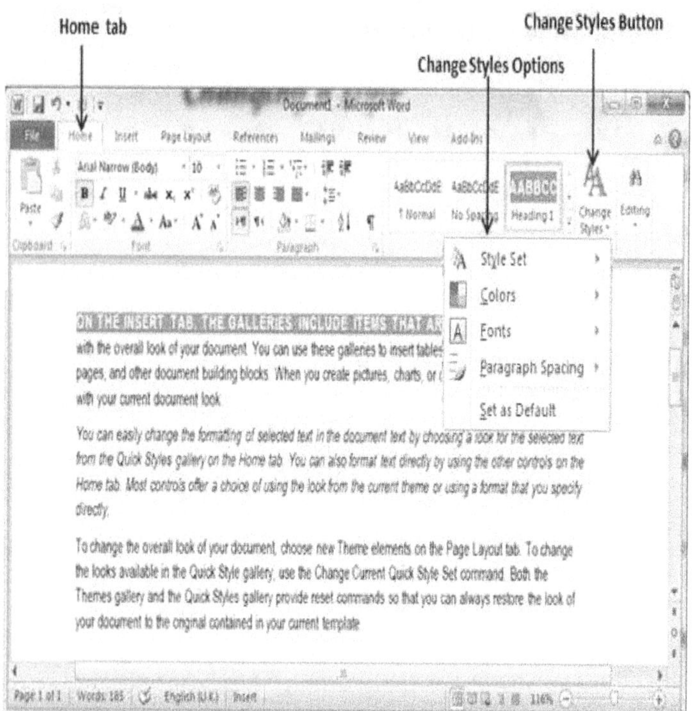

Fig. 3

To change the style,

 click style set which will then display a submenu, so you can select from the available options. Moving the mouse over the available styles a real time text preview is displayed that gives you the idea of what you expect as the end results with the new style. See fig. 4

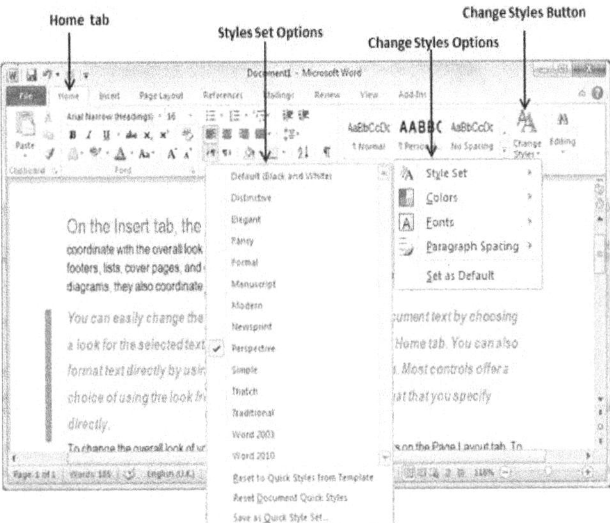

Fig. 4

iii.   To apply the selected style,

iv.   Click the selected style, your selected text changes to the new style. Look at fig.5 below

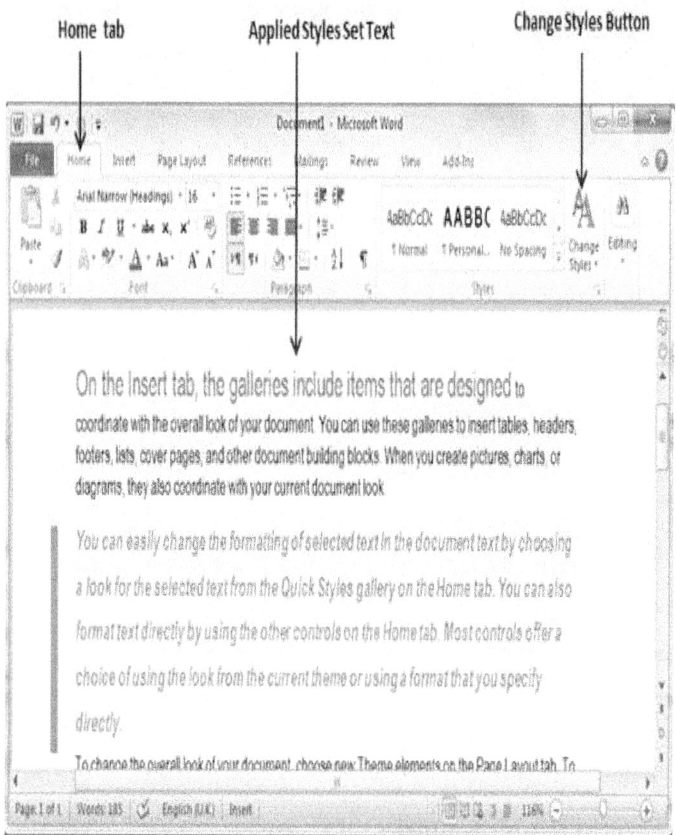

Fig, 5

b.   Creating the table of content

To add a table of content, consider a document with many subheadings. Group this subheading into various levels of headings as shown in fig. 6 below.

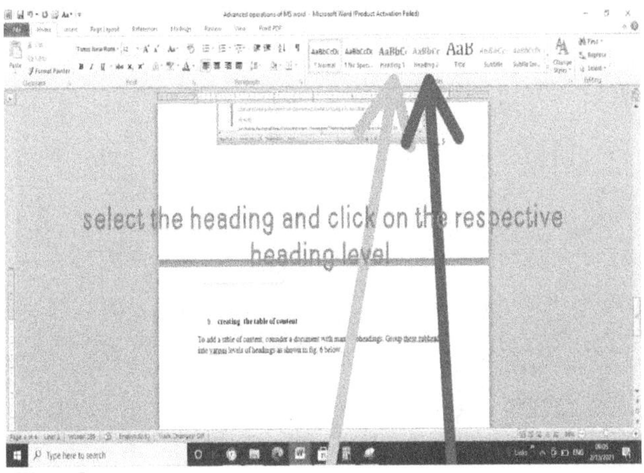

Fig. 6

When you have selected all the heading levels, whatever remains is adding the table of content. To add the table of content, click reference tab on the home tab (Home>reference) then the table of content button. Select the format of the table of content you like from the list, click on that format. See fig. 7 below

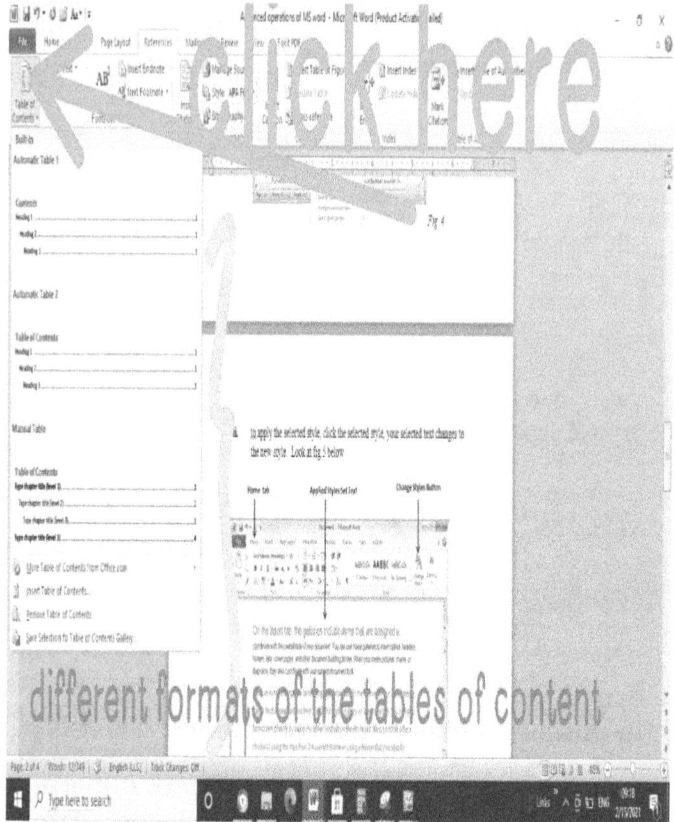

Fig. 7

select the number of levels of headings

You can further select the number of levels of headings you need in your table of content. Click insert table of content available on the menu below the table of content format (see fig. 8a). A dialogue box will appear with different levels of headings as shown in fig. 8b

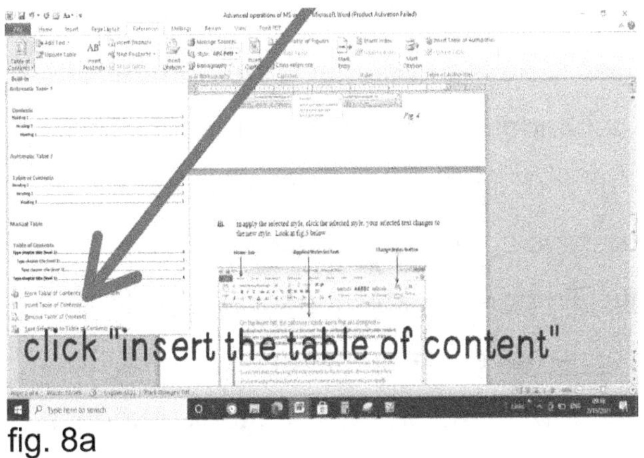

fig. 8a

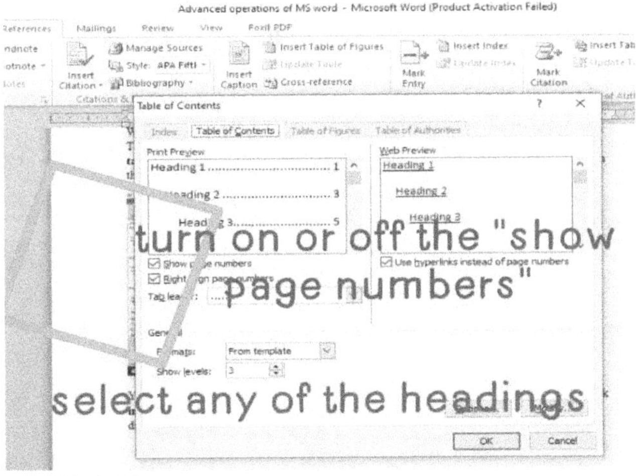

Fig. 8b.

You can turn on or off the **show page numbers** option. See fig. 8b above. When done, click **OK** to apply the changes.

Updating the table of content

As you work on the document, the number of pages continues increasing and the content vary with what you have on the table of content. Thus, there is a need of updating the table of contents. To do so, follow the following stages: You already have a table of content. Click the reference tab, then, click update table button. A display of the Update Table of contents appears in a dialogue box with two options. Look at fig. 9a and b below.

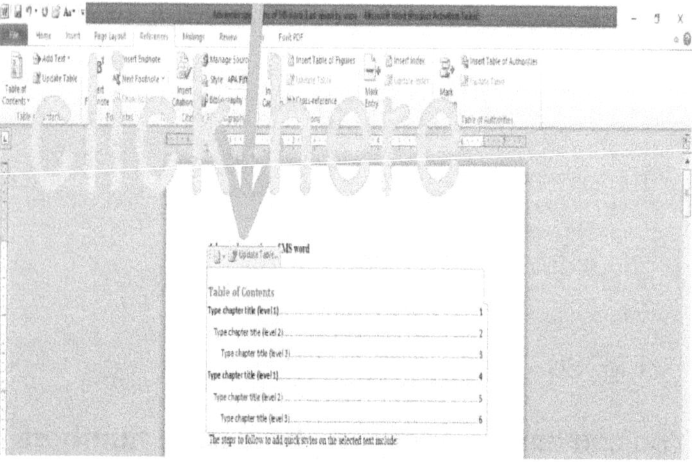

fig. 9a

fig. 9b

To update the page numbers only,

Select the first option, select update page numbers only displaying in the dialog box and if you want to update the whole table, click update entire table. This will update the entire table of content with the new information you wanted captured.

Click the reference tab; next, the table of content button to display the table of content, remove table of content option is available at the bottom. See fig. 10 below

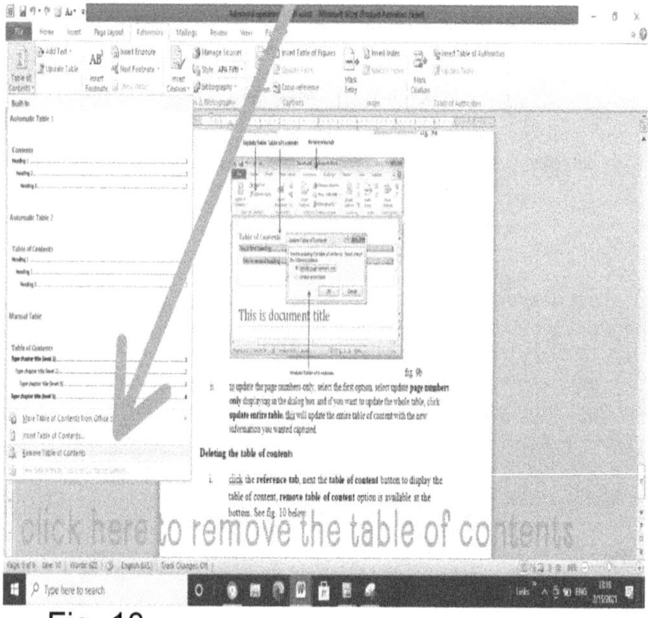

Fig. 10

Click on the Remove Table of content to delete the existing table of content.

Setting water marks

To set the watermark, follow the following steps:
Open the document you wish to add the watermark
Click page layout tab then click watermark button. A list of standard watermarks is displayed. See fog. 11 below

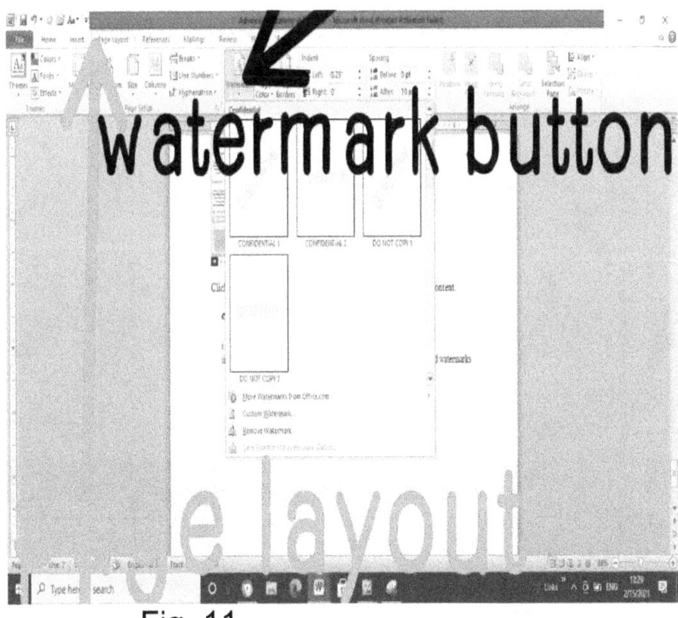

Fig. 11

Select any of the available standard watermarks by clicking on it. The watermark is applied on the entire pages in the document. e.g. if we select the confidential template, the results will be as shown in fig. 12

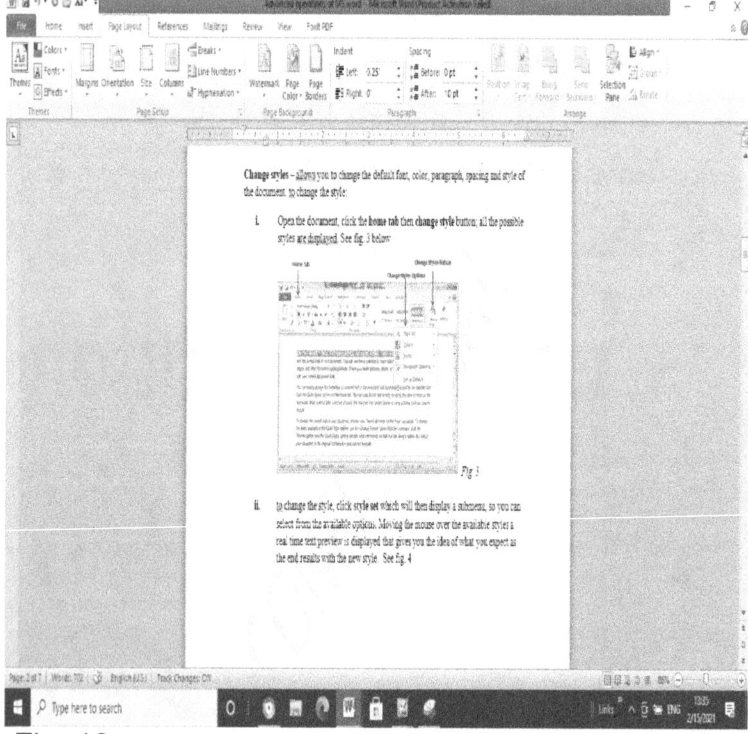

Fig. 12

Setting custom watermark

To modify the watermark to your desired taste (color, size and font), take the following steps:

a. Open the document you wish to add watermark Click the page layout tab and then click watermark. At the bottom, there is a custom watermark button. See fig. 13a below

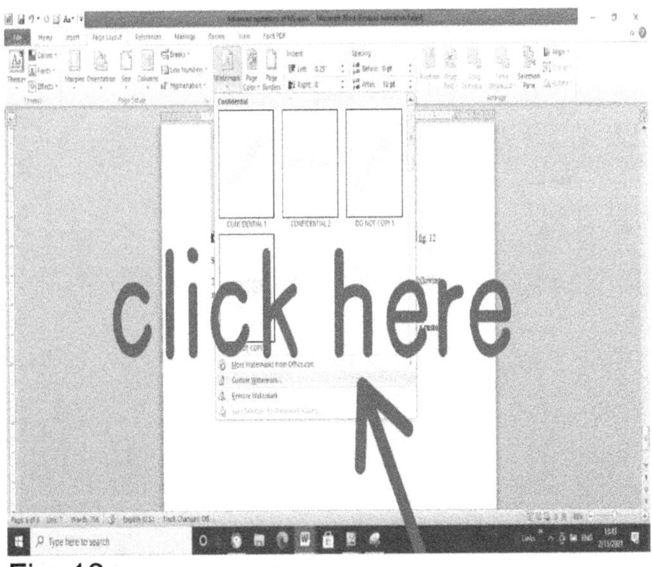

Fig. 13a

Click on the custom watermark option, a printed
display watermark dialog will appear. Look at fig.
13 b

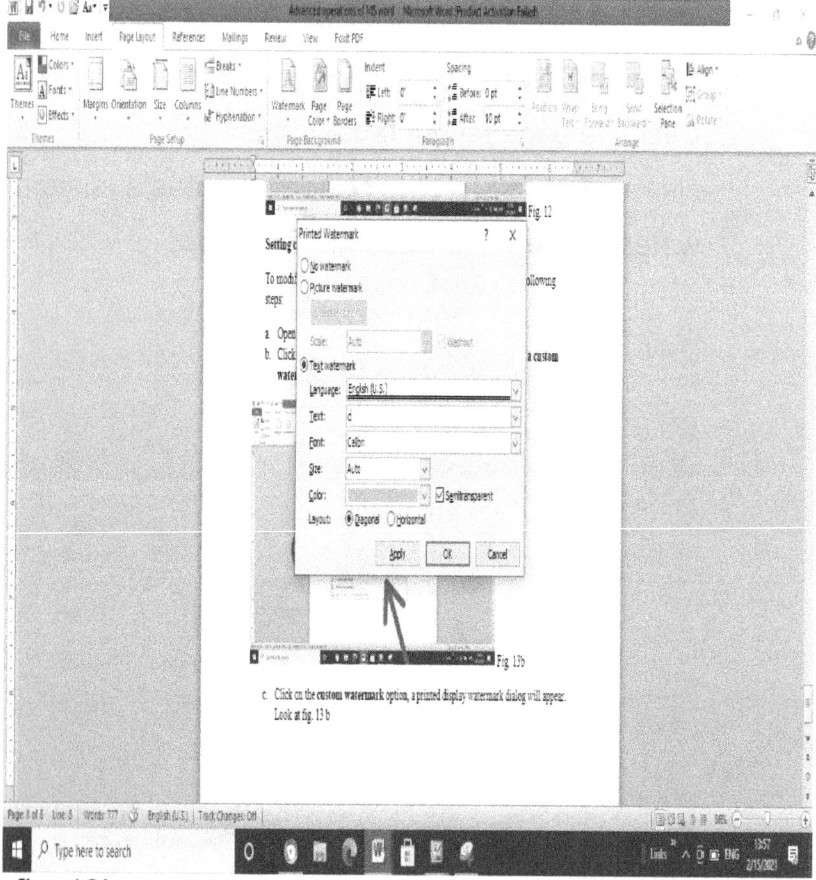

fig. 13b

set a picture as watermark

You can set a picture as watermark, just click picture watermark and you will be directed to select from your files, or you can set a predefined text watermark, click text watermark, a dialog box appears where you type the text you wish to be the watermark. For instance, let us try the word DUPLICATE then set its font size and color after all that is done, click OK. See fig. 13 c and 13 d

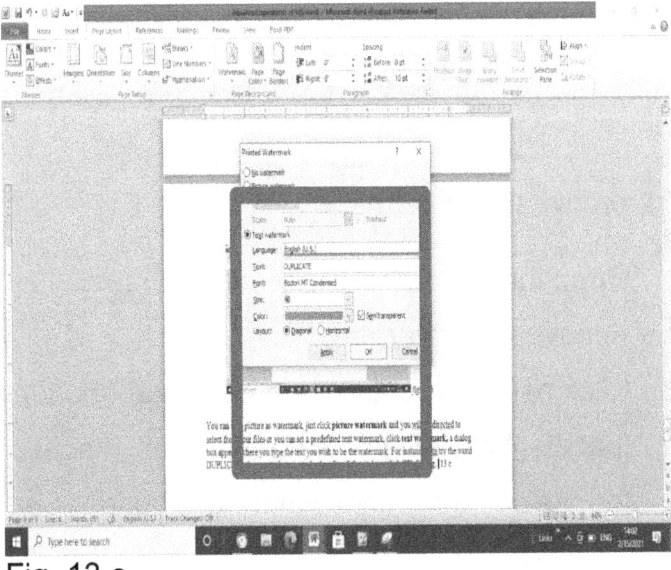

Fig. 13 c

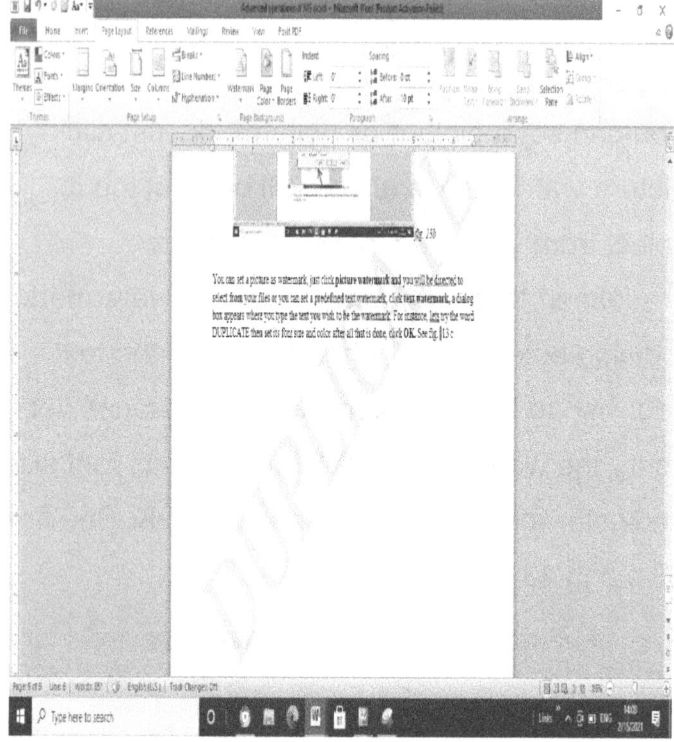

Fig. 13 d

To remove the watermark

1. Open the word document you wish to remove the watermark

2. Click page layout tab then watermark button that displays a list of watermark options, at the bottom is remove watermark button. See fig. 14 below

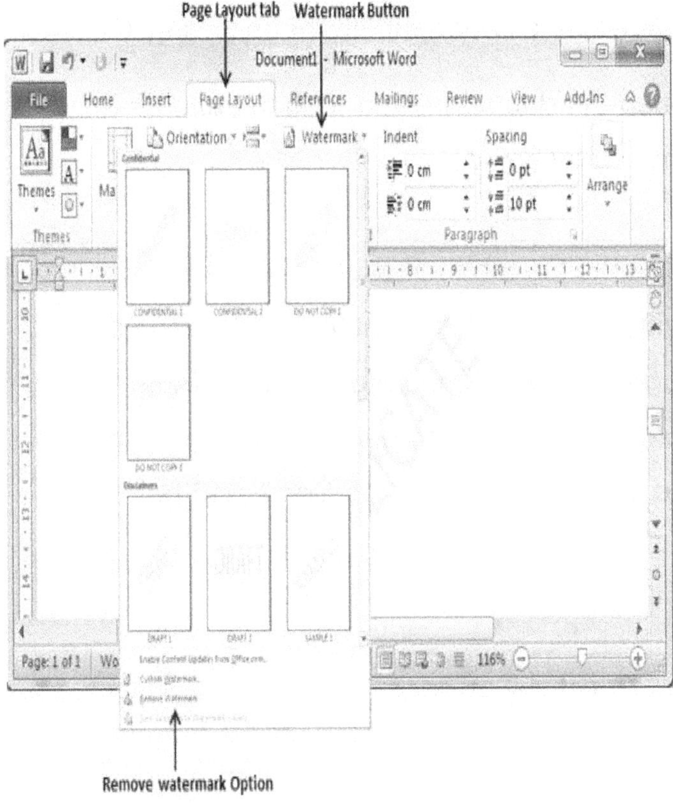

Fig. 14

Click remove watermark option, this will delete the already added watermark.

Mailing documents

To send a word document was an attachment to a given email address, do the following:

Open the document you wish to send as an email attachment

Click the file tab then click save & send option available at the left most top column. A number of options will come up upon clicking the button, select send using email, an option available in the middle of the column. See fig 15 below.

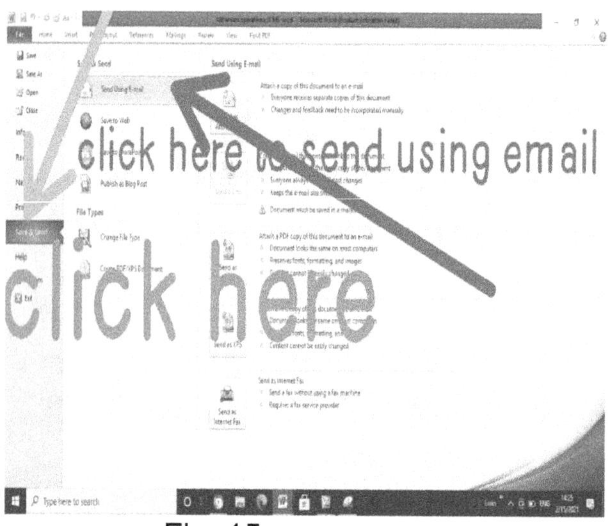

Fig. 15

In the third column, there are various options to send the email. For instance, you could send the document in DOC format or PDF format. When you click send as PDF or send as DOC, a dialog box is displayed that allows you to type the email address that you wish to send the document to, allows you to add the subject of the email and add any message you wish. To send the email to a multiple recipients, add those emails separated by semicolon (;) and a space.

b. translating the document using word translator

Click the review tab then translate button. Look at fig. 16a below

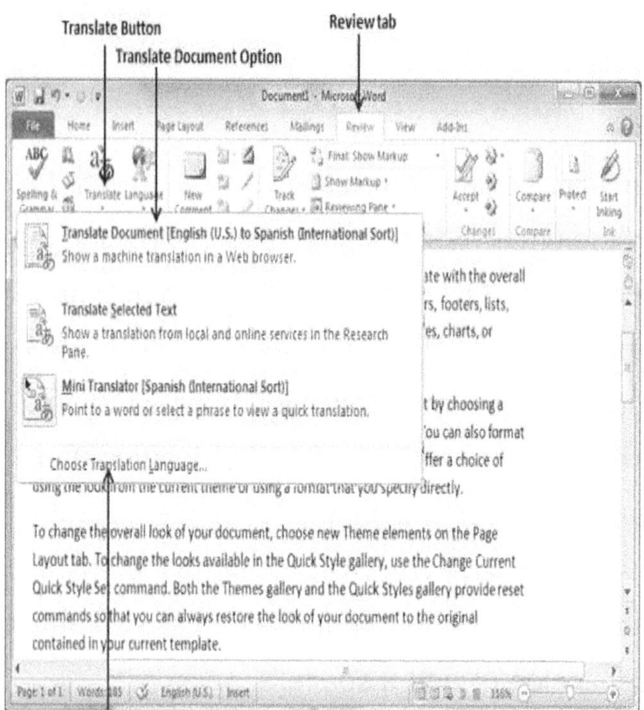

Fig. 16 a

Select the choose translation language option click on it.

You will see a display of Translation Language Options dialog box. select from the list the language you want. See fig. 16b

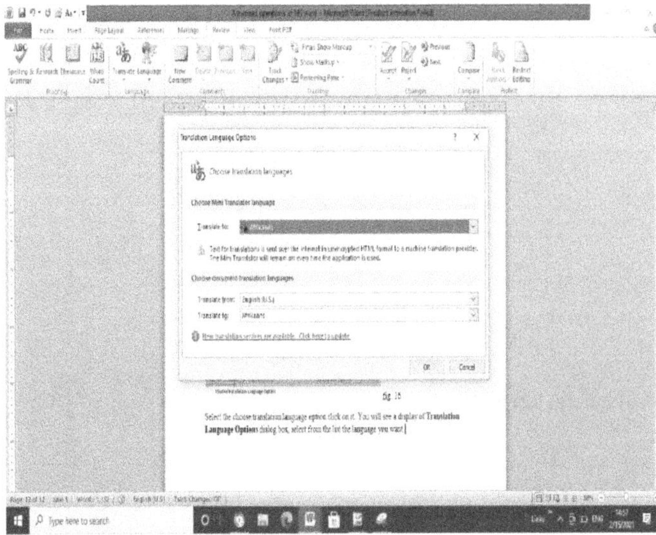

Fig. 16 b

After selecting the from language, and To Language press OK.

Get back to the Review tab and click translate button. Select top option Translate Document option from the given options, this will display Translate Whole Document dialog box asking for your permission to send your document over the internet to be translated by Microsoft Translator.

Page Orientation

Portrait: Landscape:

Setting page orientation

1st Click Page Layout

2nd Click Orientation

3rd Select one

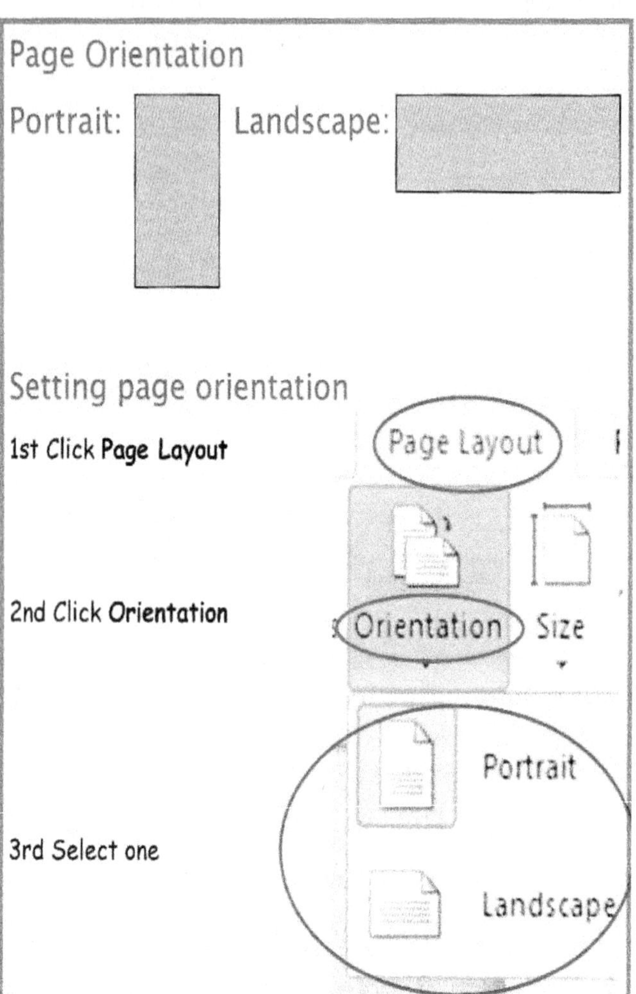

Set Page Margins

1st Click Page Layout on toolbar

2nd Click Margins

3rd Click Custom Margins

4th You now see options

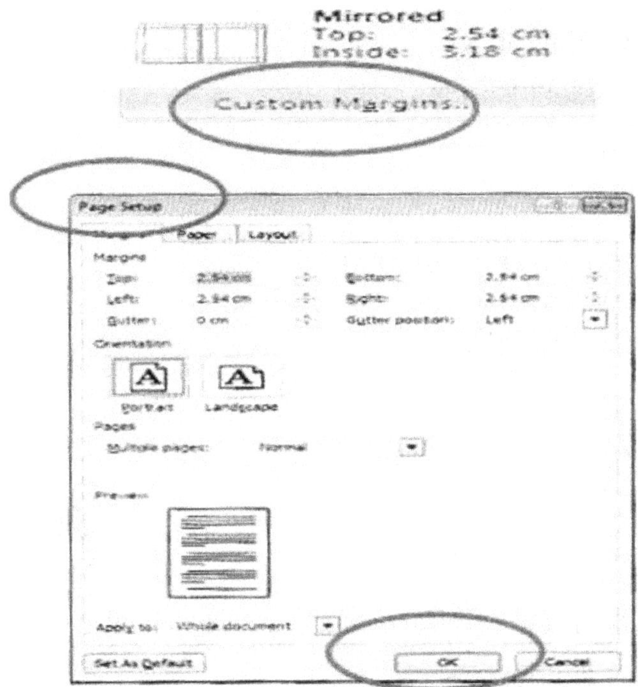

Set Header 0r Footer

First click INSERT

 Then select Header or Footer

3rd select Style

4th Type text in your footer

Text Alignment

Left   Centre   Right
Justified

Left of page Centre of page Right of page

Across entire page

1st Press left mouse and drag

across text

 2nd Click one of the

alignments above

Font choices

1st Press left mouse and drag across text

2nd Click down-arrow on Font

Drop-Down box
3rd Click on your choice
that appears

<u>Font size</u>

1st Press left mouse and drag

across text

2nd Click down-arrow for Font

sizes menu

3rd Click on a size of your

choice

Font: Bold, Italic, Underline (**B I U)**

1st Press left mouse and drag

across text

2nd Click B for bold

3rd Click / for *Italic*

4th Click U for Underline

Create a folder to put your file into

Right click on desk top

Choose new

Choose folder

Your new folder appears

2nd Type your folder name

Move folder to Address Bar

4th New folder now appear in the Address Bar

Note: Address Bar shows the folder your
document is in

Navigate to Word application document

1st Double-click

Open a new Microsoft Word document

2nd Double-click   You now see a blank page

i Microsoft Word 2010

You now see all applications

Font colour

1st Press left mouse and drag across text

2nd Click font colour Down-Arrow

3rd You now see colour options

4th Click on a colour

Line spacing: Increase/Decrease

1st Press **left mouse**

 and drag across text

2nd Click Paragraph **Down-Arrow**

3rd Select your choices

 4th Click **OK**

Heading HI /H2

1st Press left mouse and

 drag across text

2nd Click H o m e

3rd Click Heading 1 AaBbC' | AaBbCc
             Heading 1 Heading 2

Note: Heading 1—is for main title

Note: Heading 2—is for sub-title (repeat for Heading
       2)

Insert Table

1st Double-click on page where you want

table to appear

2nd Click Insert

3rd Click Table

4th Press left mouse and drag

across some of the squares

Or highlight the number of rows and column

And click on the page

Columns

1st Click Page Layout

2nd Click Columns

3rd Click Two (columns

Insert Pictures

1st Double-click on page where you want picture to appear

2nd dick insert

3rd Click Picture You now see options

4th Click on Pictures folder menu if it's not already selected

5th Double-click on Pictures folder

i Double-click your picture

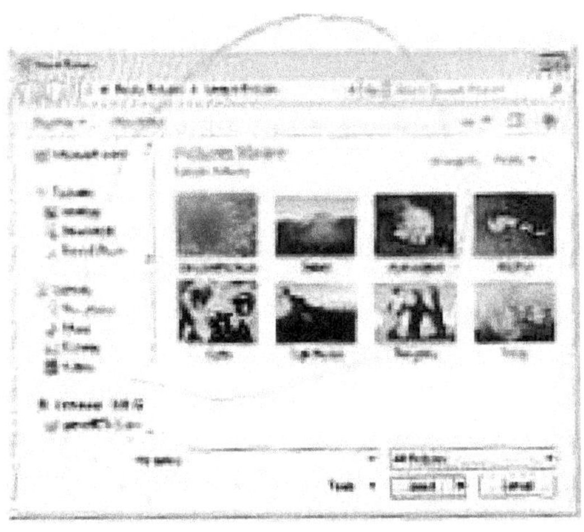

Spell-check

1st Click Review-

2nd Click

Spelling options now appear

Spelling &

Grammar

Spelling

3rd Select your choices

4th Click Cancel

Find and replace

First click Home

2nd Click Find Navigation

Pane appears

3rd Type search word

4th Click ^ Replace

Option now appear

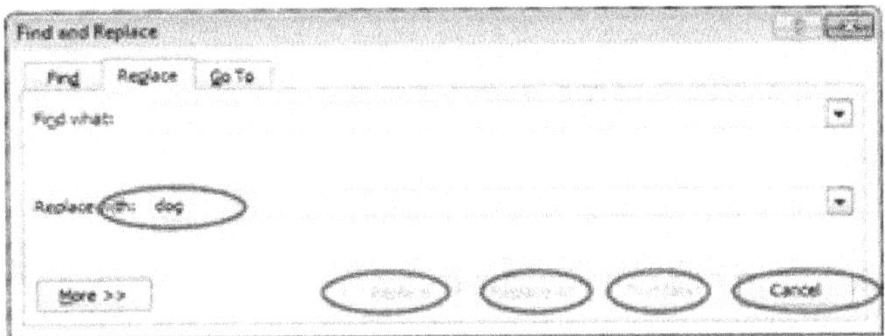

5th Type your *-preferred* word e.g. dog

6th Click Replace: Replaces one *"fox"* to "dog"

7th Click Replace All: Replaces all *"fox"* to "dog"

8th Click Find Next: Finds next occurrence of "fox" 9th Click *Cancel*:

Undo / redo

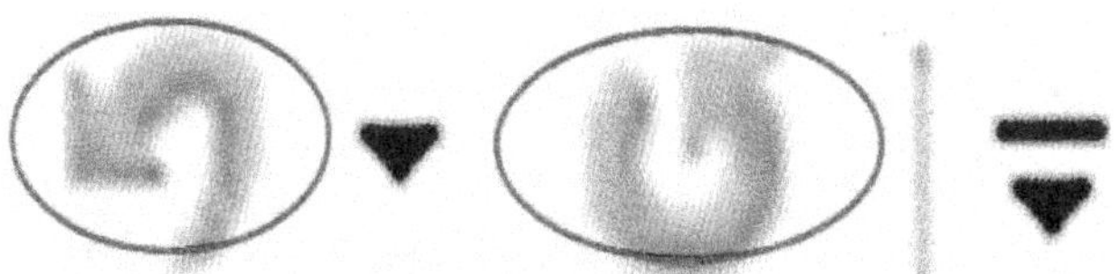

Printing

1st Click File

2nd Click Print

3rd Select your choices

4th Select copies

5th Double-click Printer icon

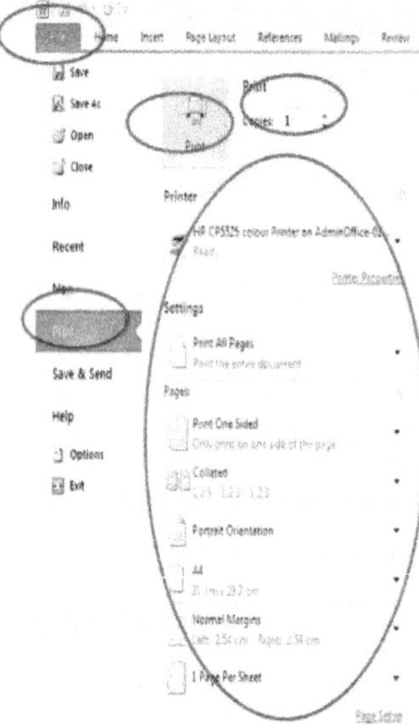

New Document

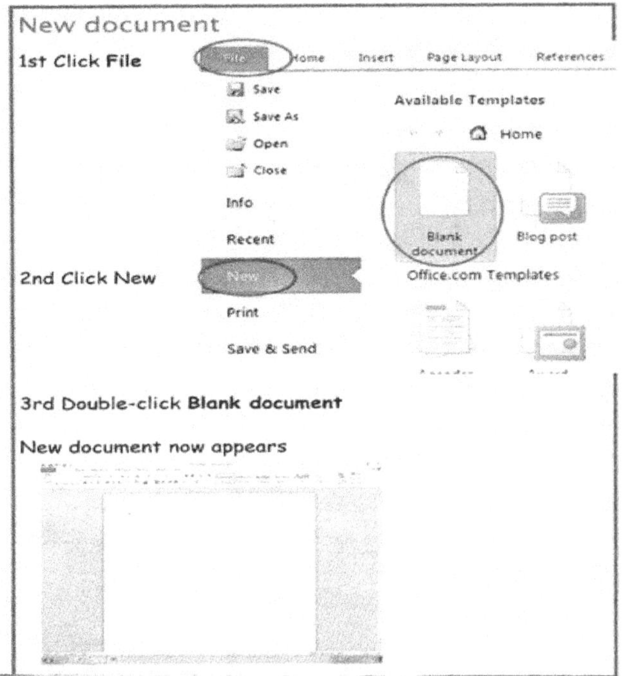

Save regularly

1st Click **File**

2nd Click Save

Note: This makes sure your work is saved in the event

of

computer error or power cut

Shut computer down OR log Off

1st Click

2nd Click

3rd Click Start Button

Bottom-left of screen

Top-right of screen)

4th Click Shut down OR Click Shut down arrow

AND select

Log off

Switch

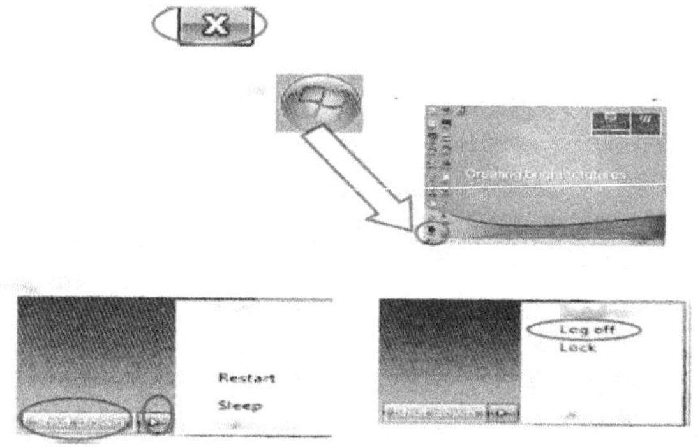

Switch computer screen off

Create Your Own Text Style

1 Click **Home**

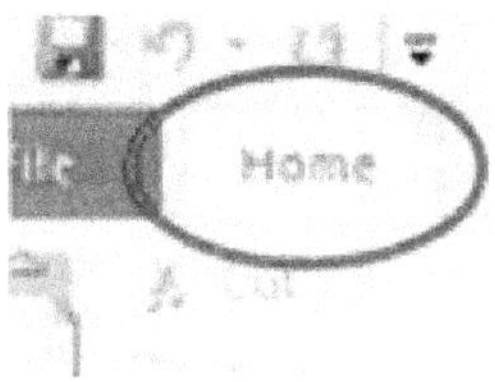

3 Click **New Style** icon

4 Click inside Name: dialogue box and type a new name

5 Click Ok

How to Use the New Style

1 Press left mouse and drag over text to highlight it

2 Click on your new style in the ribbon

The highlighted text now changes to your newly named style e.g. named "Progress"

Add More Lines to Borders

1 Right-mouse click on border line

of the text box

2 Click Format Shape

Formatting options appear

3   Click Line Style

4   Click Width: increase/decrease arrow to

select

thickness of boarder (e.g. 6.5pt)

5   Click Compound type: drop-down arrow

and click on a line style

6   6 Click Close

7   Your text box now has additional lines

(6.5pt thickness

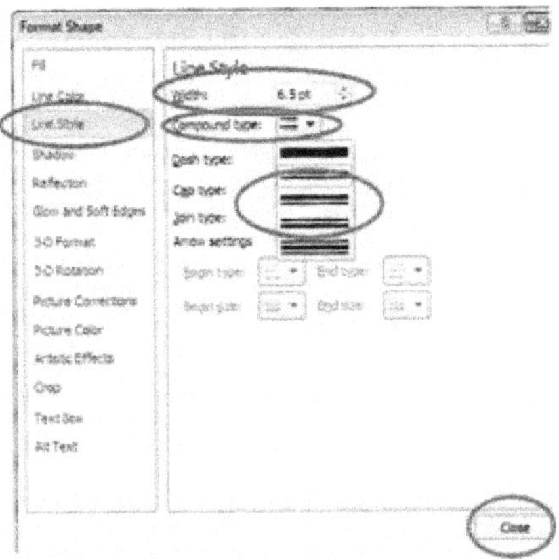

Resize Picture

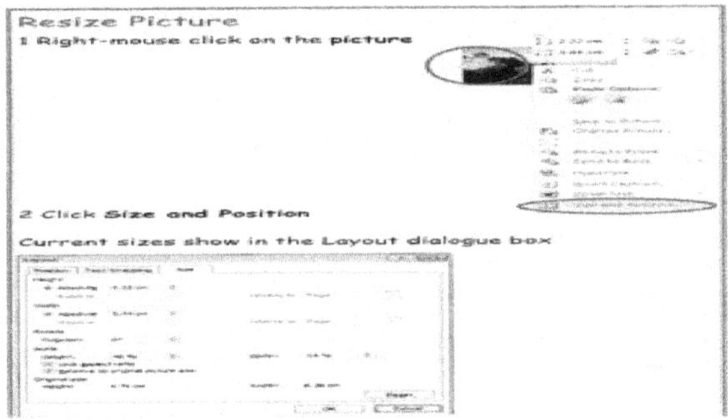

3   Click Size tab

4   Select your choices from: Height/Width/Lock

aspect

Ratio

5. Click OK

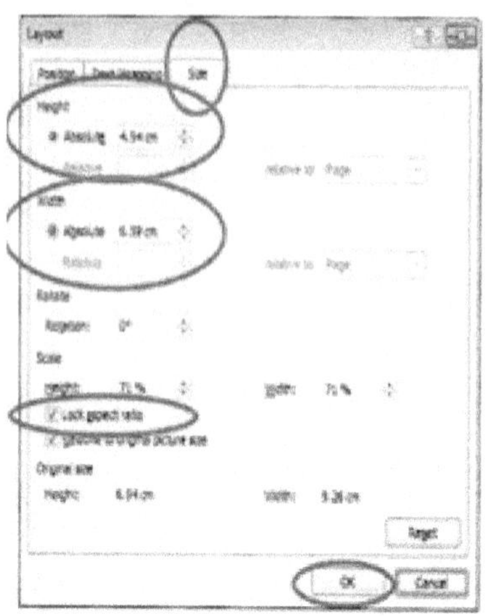

The picture is now enlarged/decreased

Note: Lock Aspect ratio

keeps the picture in

proportion when it is

resized using any corner

crop handle

Cropping Pictures

1   Right-mouse click on the picture

2   Click the Crop icon

The picture appears with crop handles around the picture

3 Hold left mouse & drag any one of the crop

handles

towards the centre of the picture and let go

The picture now appears cropped at a reduced size

4 Click left mouse on any area, outside the grey cropped
area, to retain the cropped image

Note: Cropping actually cuts part of the picture away

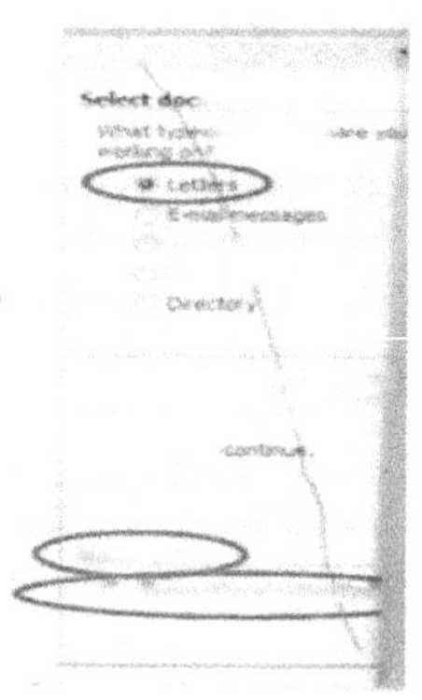

Mail Merge:

Word Merged with Excel Data Base

1 Click Mailings

2 Click Start Mail Merge

3 Click Step by Step Mail Merge Wizard.

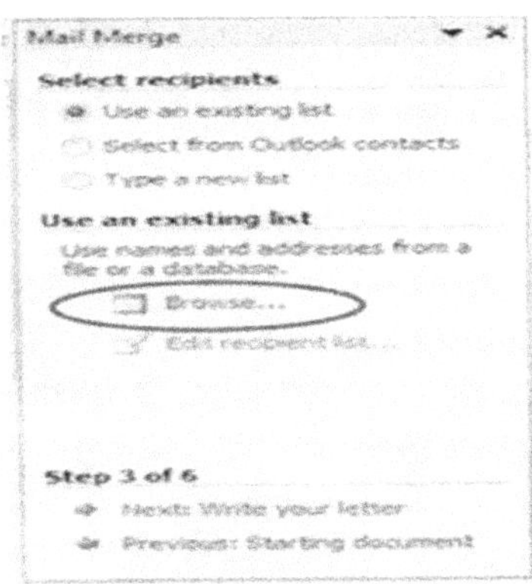

Mail Merge:

Word Merged with Excel Data Base

4 Click Mailings

5 Click Start Mail Merge

6 Click Step by Step Mail Merge Wizard.

Letters

E-mail Messages

Envelopes...

labels...

Directory

Normal Word Document

Step by Step Mail Merge

Set Pages to X of Y in Header or Footer
X = Page no. and Y = Number of pages

1 Click Insert

2 Click Page Number

3 Click Bottom of Page

4 Scroll to Page X of Y

5 Click on Page X of Y Area inside the window

The Footer now looks like this.

Footer

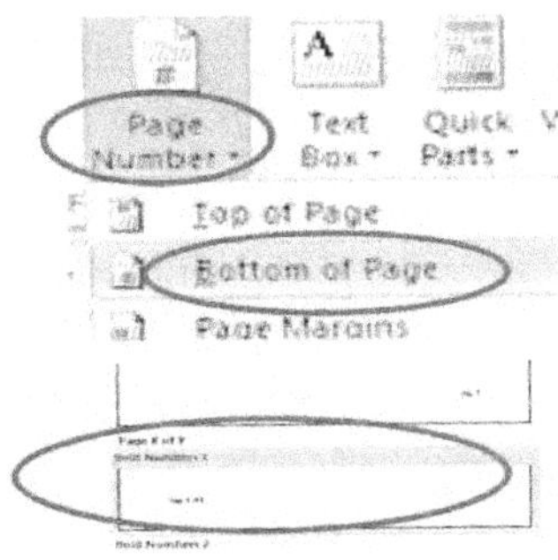

Tabs setting

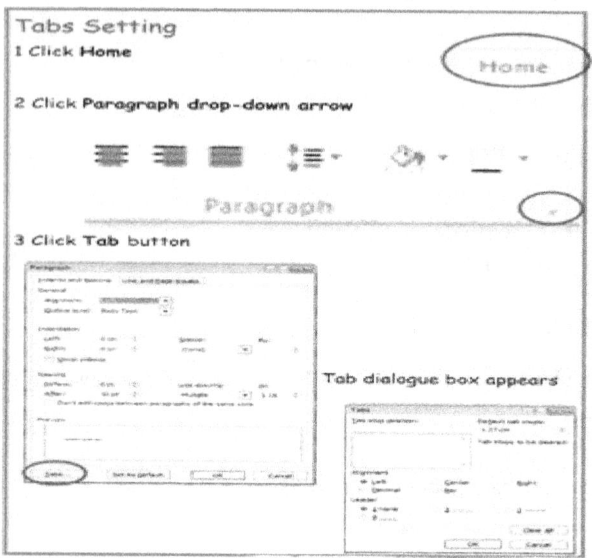

4   Click in the Tab stop position: window and type your

tab stop distance (e.g. 1.3 cm)

5   Click Set. Your tab number now moves below

Repeat for next the tab stops (e.g. 2.5 cm)

6   Click Ok

Your tab stops are now set

How to test the tab stops

7 Press the tab key (far left on the keyboard)

Your cursor now moves to the next tab stop, on

the page, each time you press the tab key

Note: You can now type at each tab stop

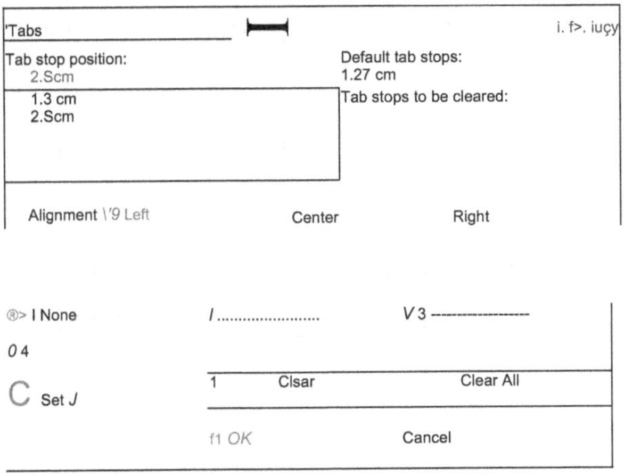

'Tabs   i. f>. iuçy

Tab stop position:	Default tab stops:
2.Scm	1.27 cm
1.3 cm	Tab stops to be cleared:
2.Scm	

Alignment \'9 Left   Center   Right

®> I None   / ....   V 3 -----------------

0 4

C Set J   1   Clsar   Clear All

f1 OK   Cancel

Chapter4

Microsoft power point (PPT) For Beginners

Definition

A software developed by designed to create
electronic presentations involving of a series of
separate pages or slides. Which convey data in
multimedia and is used to create complex
business presentations, for educational outlines
business and lot more
The power point presentation can be saved
under (JPEG, GIF, PNG, etc.), videos (WMV or
MPEG-4), or text (PDF).

Synopsis of PowerPoint

developed by Dennis Austin and Thomas Rudkin
at Forethought. Inc In August of 1987, Microsoft
bought Forethought for $14 million and turned it
into its graphics business unit, where the
company continued to develop the software. The
first iteration was launched together with
Windows 3.0 in 1990, now window 10

Power Point Screen

Power Point screen

Ribbon of Power point

Bottom of Power point

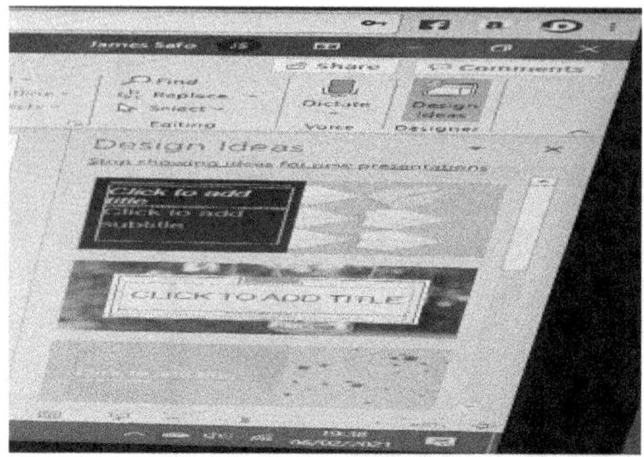

Right side of the Power point screen

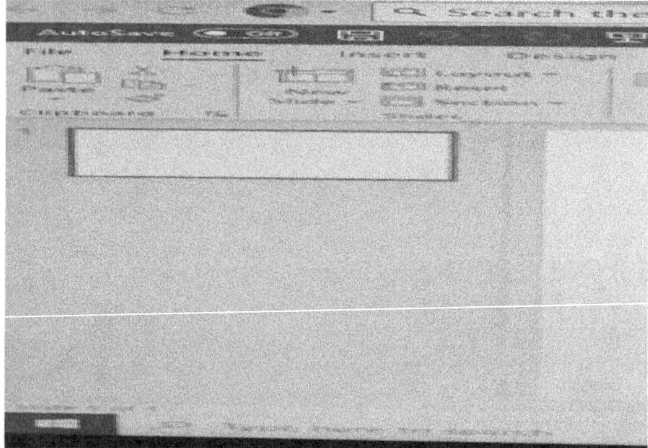

Left side of screen of PowerPoint

How to create a power point for beginner

The potential uses of PowerPoint are incalculable.

A slide show can help an instructor present a lesson, effectively show measurable data, or be utilized for corporate training. A slide show can be an important instrument for educating, sharing, and learning PowerPoint introductions are valuable regardless of the theme and help impart knowledge to a group of people. Coming up next are steps on making a basic PowerPoint presentation, however, explicit steps may fluctuate somewhat relying on the version of PowerPoint you are using.

Function

With PowerPoint on your PC, Mac or mobile device, you could:

a. Create presentations from scratch or template
b. Add text, images, art, and videos
c. Select professional design with PowerPoint Designer

d. Add transitions, animations and, motion

e. Save to one drive, so to get your presentation from your files in the tablet, iPhone, or computer.

f. share with other people wherever they are.

Step 1:

Creating / launching the PowerPoint program

Click the start and search/ click on the power point icon on your computer to open PowerPoint Select a blank presentation to create a new presentation from scratch. Select one of the templates. as shown in fig. 1 below

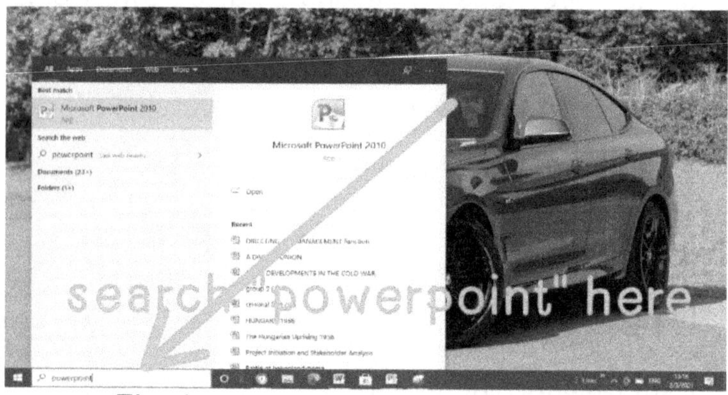

Fig. 1

After launching the PowerPoint, pick the kind of document you wish to use. Click on the template to create a new document. if the program does not ask you to choose a blank presentation, then it will be automatically launched.

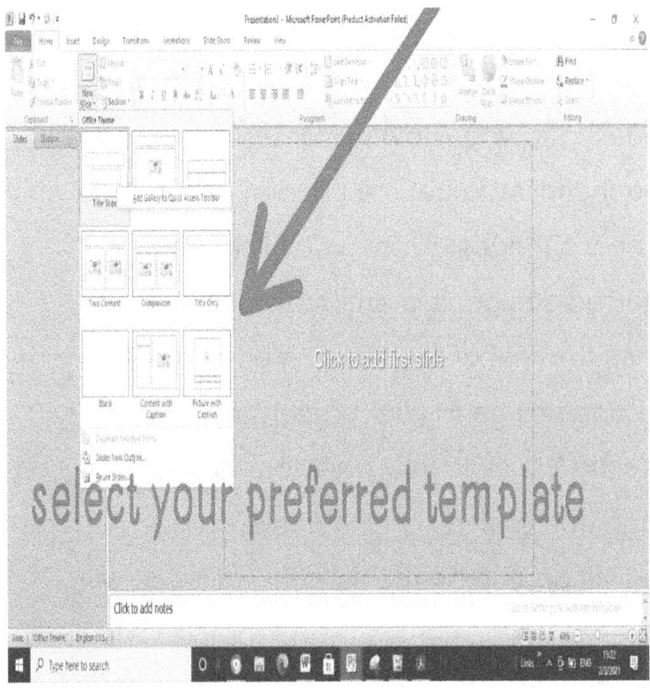

Fig. 2

Step 2:

choosing the appropriate design

You have launched the presentation; it is now time to decide what design you like for the presentation. To get the design, click on the "design" at the top of the home page. Navigate through the options to decide which design looks appealing to you. Hover over the designs that appear similar to get the preview before applying the new changes. When you click on your preferred design, it is automatically spread across the rest of the slides. You can have more than one design in your presentation by selecting the slide you want to change the design and clicking on the design you want. The slide will pop up on the screen, then you will right-click the design you want for the slide then select "apply to the selected slide. The new design will appear on the selected slide only. See fig 3

select your preferred design
Click to add title
Click to add subtitle
Click to add notes

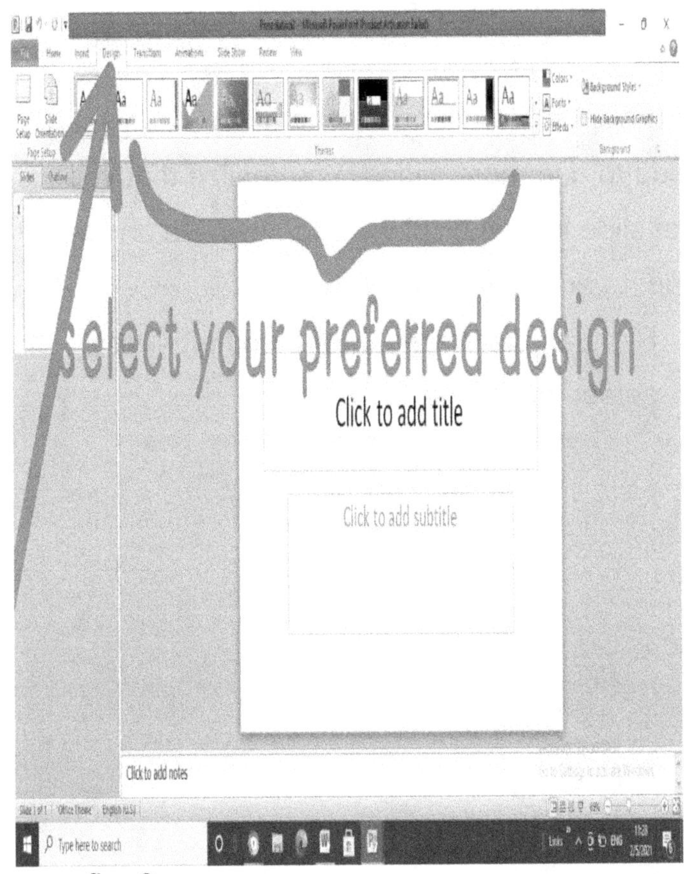

fig. 3

Step 4:

Adding more designs

You want to do a long presentation , then you'll need to add more slides. You realize that you first slide is also displayed somewhere on the left side. to add a new slide,

a. Right-click the area under the first slide, select "new slide"

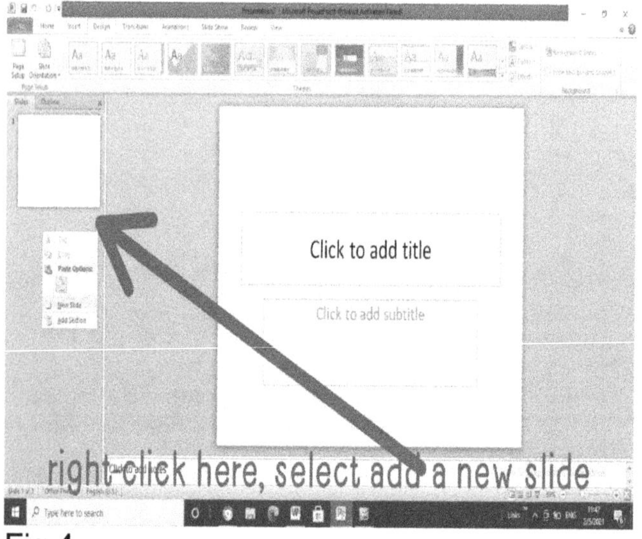

Fig 4

b. Click "new slide" on the toolbar above the slides. This command has two functions :

The top will insert a new slide with a default layout. The bottom half allows you to choose the layout you want.

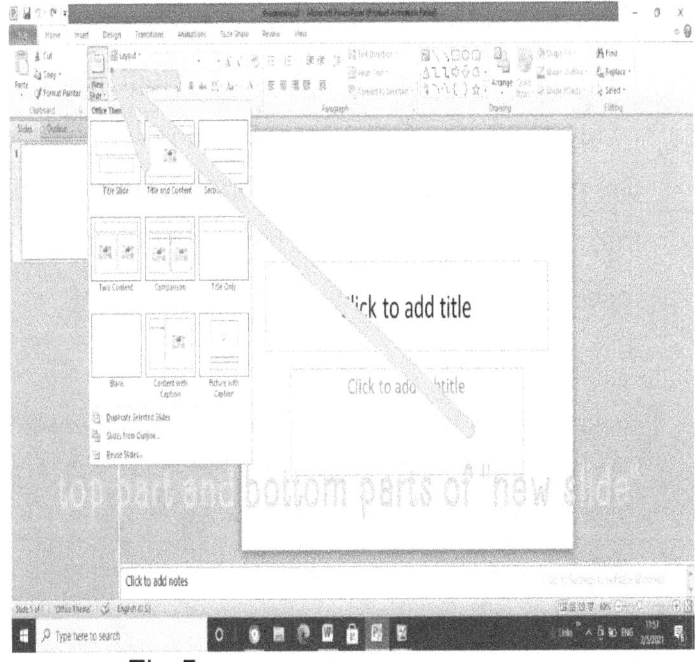

Fig 5

You can choose a slide with two textboxes and a title, one textbox, only a title, and many other options. You will see your new slide appear to the left under the first, as well become the large slide that you can edit. The design you chose earlier will be carried along in the new slides.

Step 5:

Adding charts, pictures, graphs and others

In the event that you need to embed a diagram, picture, chart, or some other graphics,

a.   click on the 'insert' tab at the highest point of the window. Here you will see catches of the multitude of choices of what you can add into your slide. Click the desired box and insert what it is you need to have on that slide

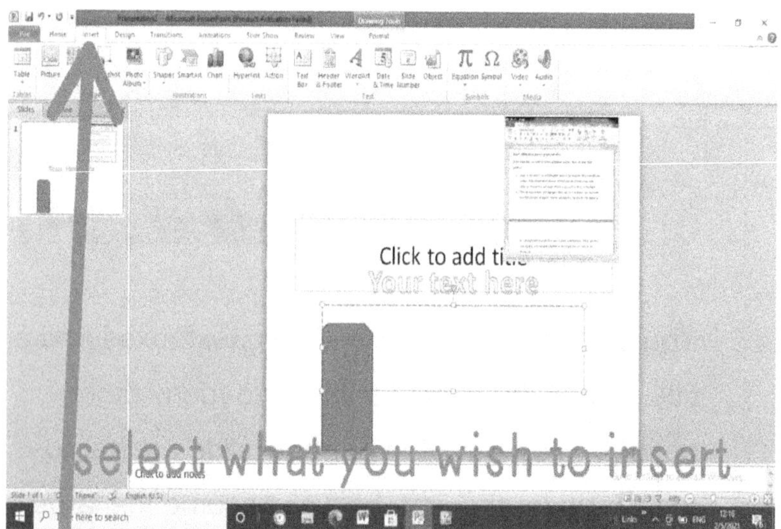

b. You can add pictures and diagrams when you have an empty box or picture box. Little photos of similar choices you found in the tool kit will appear in the container, and you can click any of these to embed also. When you have your picture, you can add a borders or alter it anyway you need in the 'format' tab.

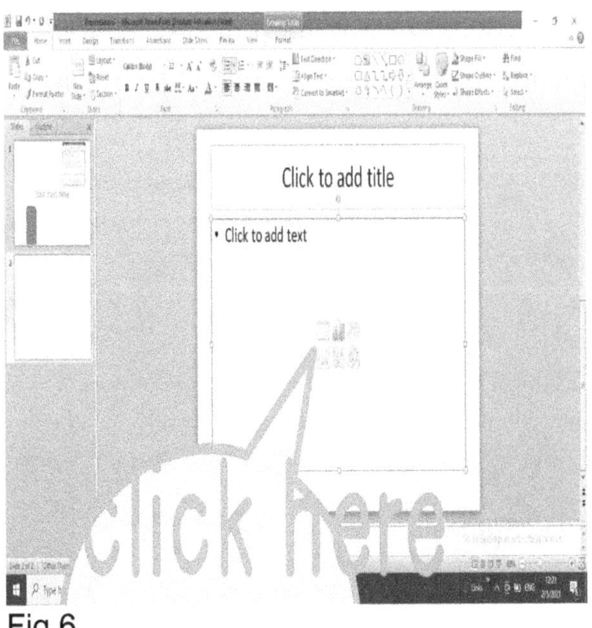

Fig 6

Step 6:

Adding transitions

To add transitions in the middle of your slides, click the 'transition' tab at the highest point of the page. Here you can look through all the choices of transitions, and drift over them to see a preview. Select the slide you need the add the transition, and afterward click the transition you picked. You can choose different transition for different slides or select same transition for all the slides.

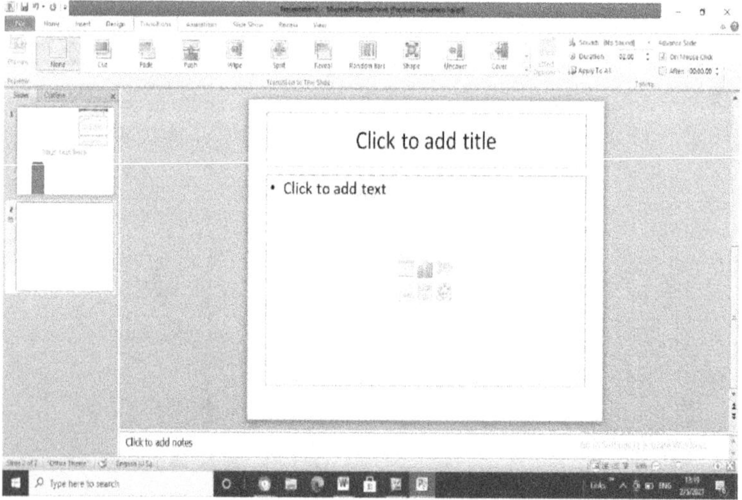

Fig 7

Step 7:

changing the order of slides

After making all the slides, you may wish change the order in which the slides appear. To do this,

a. you need to drag the slides from whether they are to where you want them in the order.

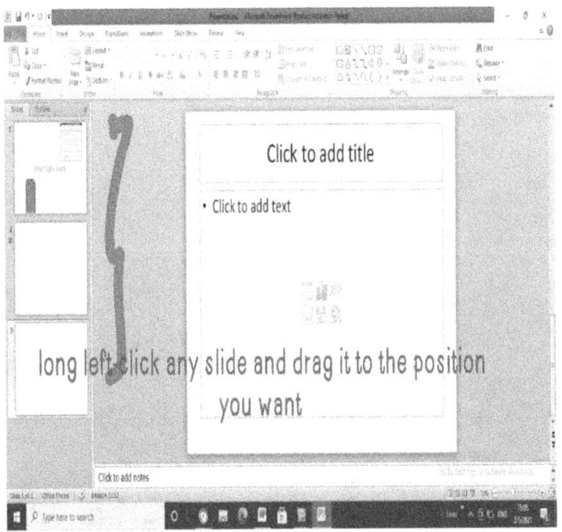

Fig 8

b. Click the "outline" icon located above in the right corner of every slide. Here, the list of all the slides so you can click and drag the slides to the order you like.

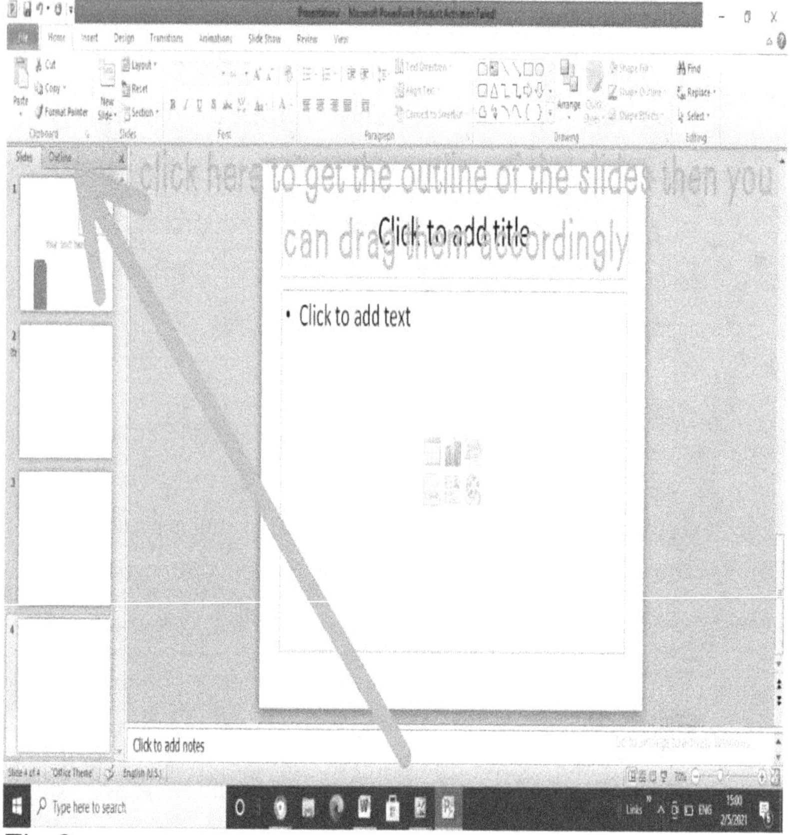

Fig 9

Step 8:

 Slide presentation

When you have each one of your slides finished and in the order you like, click "slideshow." Click the 'Slide Show' tab at the highest point of the page and select 'From Beginning'. You can review your whole slideshow and change slides by clicking or navigating with the right arrow or press F5. Congrats! You now become a PowerPoint guru!

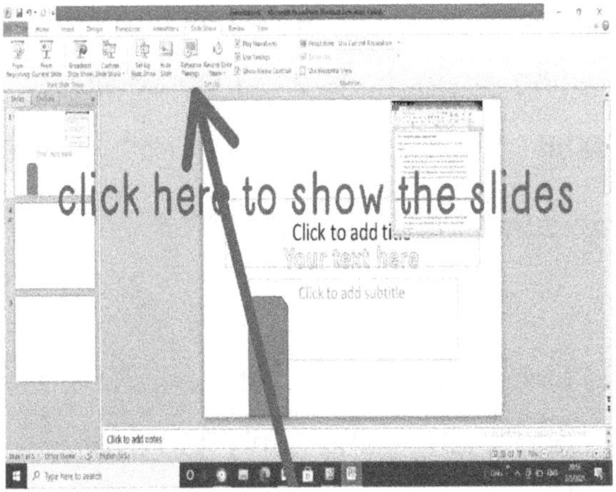

Fig 10

Chapter 5

Power Point (Microsoft) (Advance)

From the previous discussion, you know the basics of PowerPoint, starting the app, creating slides, adding designing, presenting the slides and so forth. Presented here are more instructions of using advanced features PowerPoint, including slide masters, technique for running a presentation, animations and incorporating multimedia.

1. Working with Slide Masters

Just like templates, slide masters allow one to make one change and apply it to every other slide in the presentation, including the yet to be added slides.

Before you start building individual slides, it is a good idea to create a slide master because:

When you have the slide master first, any new slide you add to your presentation will be based on the slide master.

Creating a slide master

 master after the start of building the slides may not have the desired results; some of the slides may not conform to the slide master design

To work with the slide master, go to the view tab, choose slide master. Look at fig. 1 below.

Fig 1

Alternatively, you could use the shortcut to launch the Slide Master by holding the Shift key while clicking the Normal View button located in the lower right corner of the window. Look at fig. 2 below:

Fig 2

What appears upon launching the Slide master is not the content of the slides, those slide thumbnails appearing on the left side of the window are the slide masters with each of the available slide layout. The fig. 3 above shows the layout of slide master.

Fig3

The changes made by the slide master will apply to all other slides, those already created those the ones to be created in the same layout in future. Look at fig. 4

Fig 4

All slides will appear in the like shown in fig. 4

To close the slide master view,

 click Close Master View on the slide master as shown in fig. 5 above.

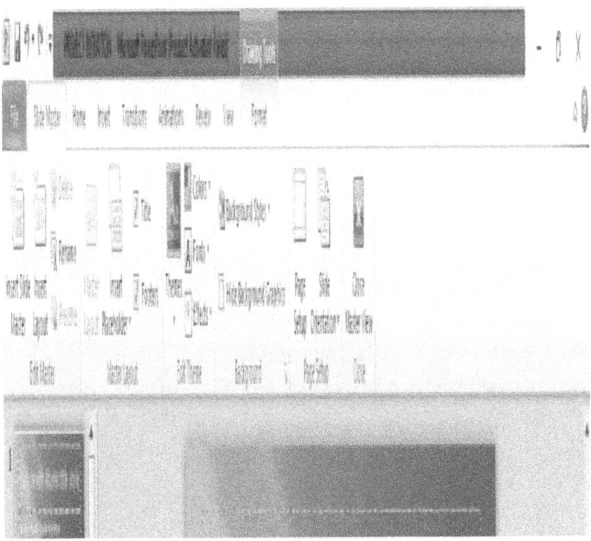

Fig 5

2. PowerPoint highlighting and pen features

While making a presentation, highlighting of key points become important. To do this, the following steps are taken:

a. In the presentation, right-click and choose pointer option. See fig. 6

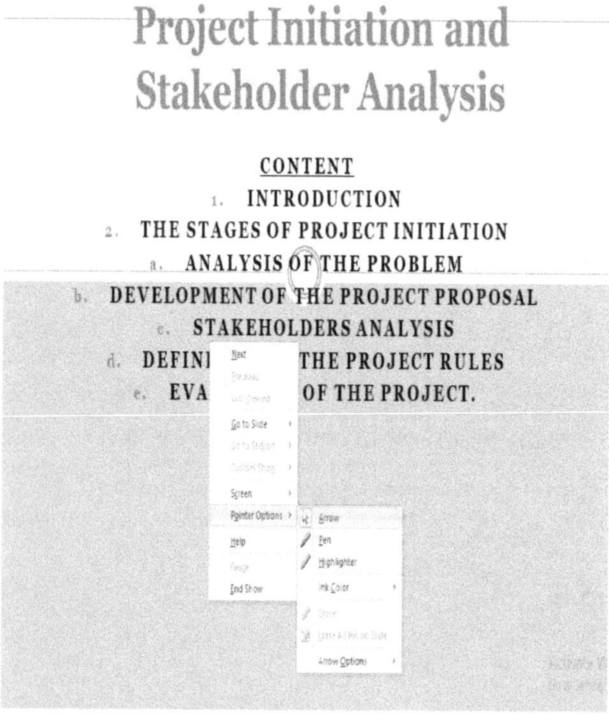

Project Initiation and Stakeholder Analysis
CONTENT
1. INTRODUCTION
2. THE STAGES OF PROJECT INITIATION
a. ANALYSIS OF THE PROBLEM
b. DEVELOPMENT OF THE PROJECT PROPOSAL
c. STAKEHOLDERS ANALYSIS
d. DEFINI THE PROJECT RULES
e. EVA OF THE PROJECT.
Next
Go to Slide
Screen
Pointer Options
Help
End Show
Arrow
Pen
Highlighter
Ink Color
Arrow Options

fig.6

i.   The ballpoint pen allows you to draw with a fine pen

ii.   Felt tip ten allows you to draw with a thicker pen

iii.   Highlighter allows you to draw with a thick pen

iv.   Ink color is used to change the color of your drawing tools. See fig. 7

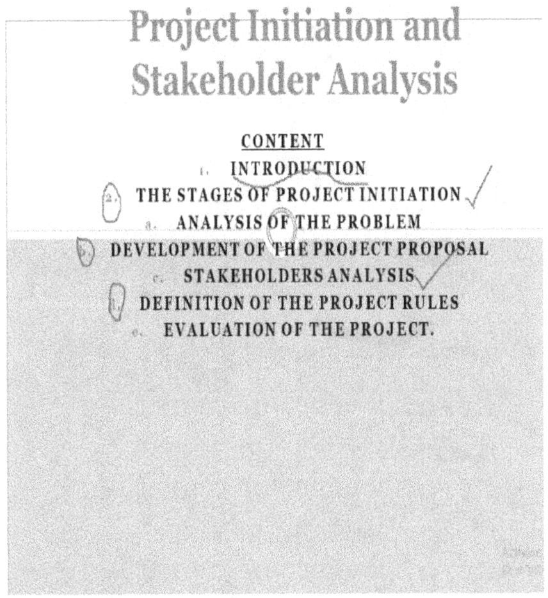

Fig. 7

Note: A multiple colours to choose, including those compliment your theme.

b. When presenting, press "E" on the keyboard if you wish to erase the drawings.

c. When you are done the presentation, you have an option of discarding the changes to keep the original content less the highlights/colors. Not that "keep" saves the drawings and they will appear next time you make the slide show. "Discard" removes the drawings. Look at fig.8 below

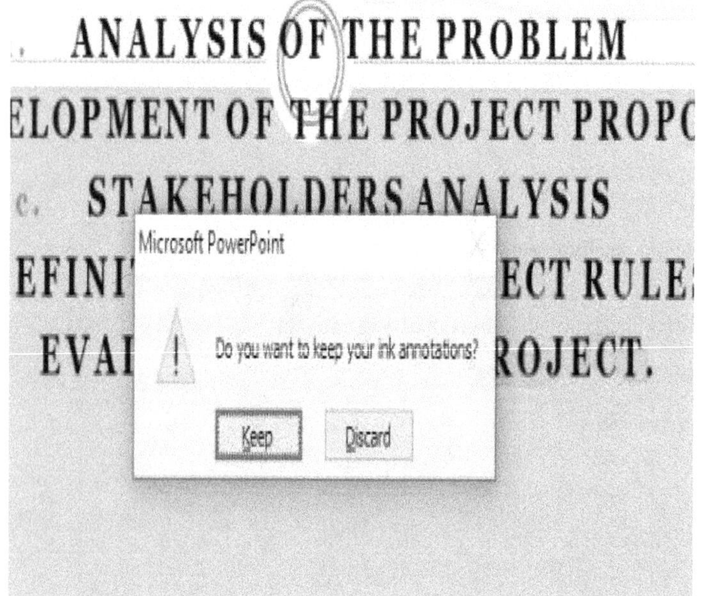

Fig. 8

d. To refocus the attention of the audience to you away instead of the slides, use button "B" on the keyboard to turn the screen black. Alternatively, you can press "W" key on the screen to turn the screen white. Press the respective button a second time to return to the slide presentation.

e. When making a presentation, use a wireless mouse where possible so that you are not tied to one position.

Using animation

Animations give your presentation sound, visual effects, or movement. Animations are also used when focusing at very important points to control the flow of information; may be to increase the viewer's interest.

Applying the animations

a. Select the text or object you want to animate.

b. Go to the animations tab, in the animations group select the animation you want. See fig. 9 below

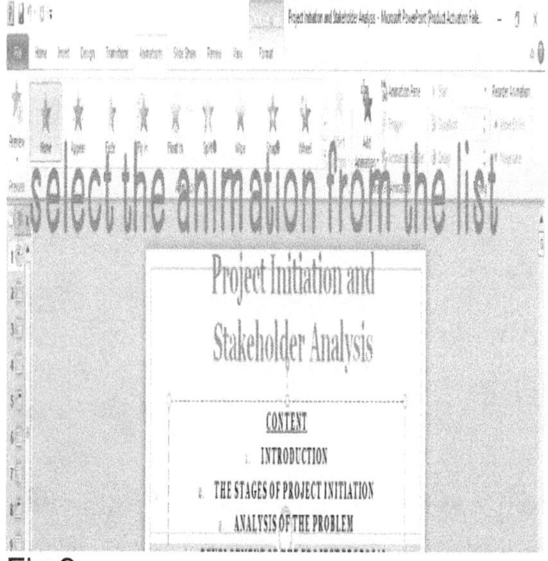

Fig 9

To take control over how your animation appears, and the effects on the animations, you can create and apply customer animations. Customized animations can be created from Custom animation task pan by following the following steps:

i.   Select the object or text you wish to animate

ii.   Go to the animations tab, in the animations list select custom animation.

iii.   An animation task pane pops on the right side of the window. See fig. 10 below

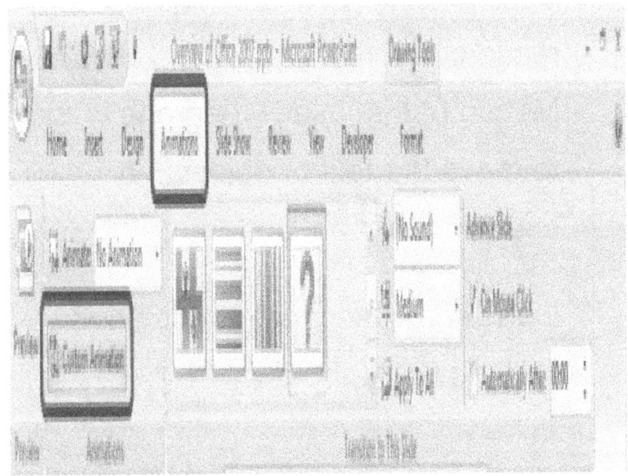

Fig. 10

iv.   Click add effect button and select the effect you like. Look at fig 11

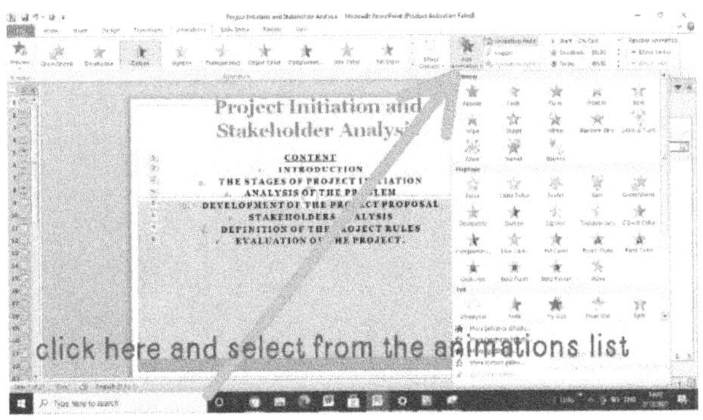

Fig 11

There are four types of effects that are worth knowing. These are:

i. Entrance- used to usher the document or object to the screen.

ii. Emphasis- added to an object that is already visible on the screen.

iii. Exit- used to make the object or text move out of the screen.

iv. Motion paths- used when one wants to move the text or object in a specific direction/ pattern.

Icons show the type of animation. Look at fig. 12 below:

Fig 12

Modification of animation effect.

c. You can modify the time of animation effects. The timings could be:4

i. Start on click- when you begin the slide, the animation effects roll out.

ii. Start with the previous- where the new animation begins at the same time as the previous effect.

iii. Start after previous- the animation begins after the previous animation is done playing. Look at fig.13 below

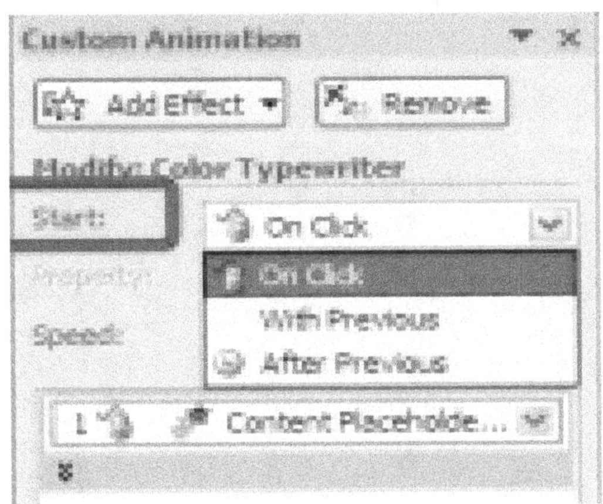

Fig. 13

iv.   You could also set the speed of the animations. See fig. 14 below

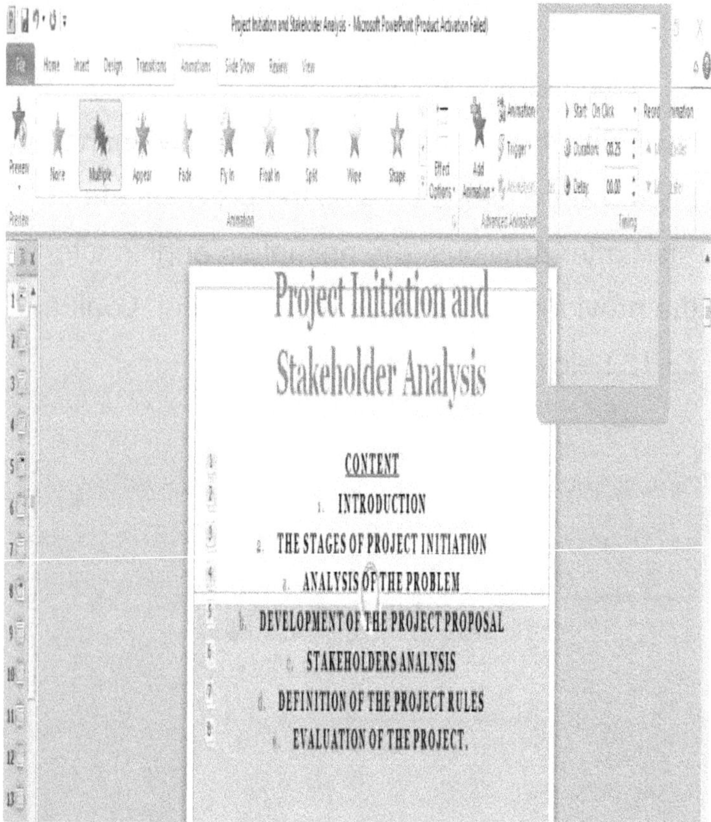

Fig. 14

Incorporating media

PowerPoint allows us to add sound or movie clips in your slides. If links were used, there could be possible problems by some not opening and the audience missing the audio or visual aspects you had wished in your presentation. Thus, it becomes a good idea to copy the sound or video clip into the presentation. To insert sound and video clip, follow the above procedure:

a. Click the insert tab on the left top corner of the window.
b. Click allow sound, a function available at the media group. See fig. 15 below

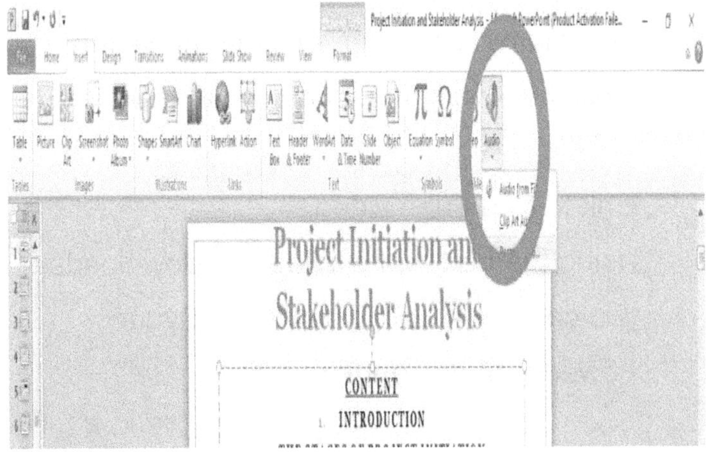

Fig. 15

Do the following to add the sound/ audio

1. Click sound from file, locate the folder with the sound you wish to add, and then double click that file.

2. Click sound from clip organiser, navigate in the clip art task pane to select the clip you wish to insert, click it to add in the slide.

3. To play the sound from the cd, click play CD audio track.

4. To record the sound, click record sound to use a microphone to record yourself as you present.

c. There are available features in the sound tools tab that can be used to customize the sound options. For instance, you can adjust the volume. However, this feature is only available when the sound clip is selected.

Link to You Tube video
Using the free-add available in downloads; you can link a YouTube video in your PowerPoint presentation.

a. Download the add-in from
http://presentationsoft.about.com/od/powerpoint2
007/ss/071213youtube07.htm

b. After downloading and installing the add, a
YouTube video tab will pop on your tool pane.
See fig. 16 below

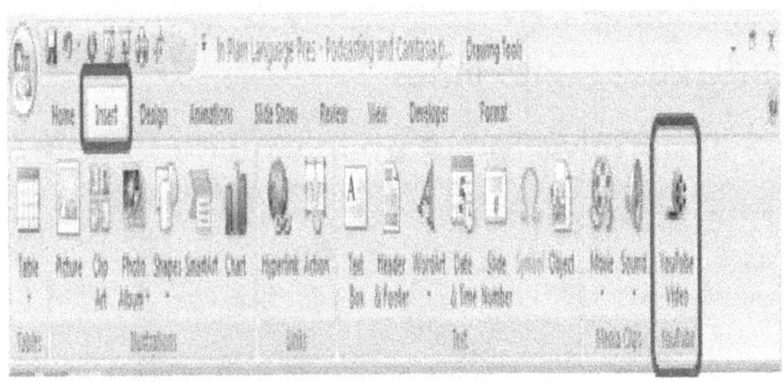

Fig 16

c. Click the YouTube video tab to start the app, the
app will navigate you the steps until you have
the intended YouTube video linked to your
PowerPoint presentation.

Note:

You must have internet connection to watch a
YouTube video in your PowerPoint presentation.
The YouTube video is not embedded to the
PowerPoint slides but linked on the web.

Chapter 7

EXCEL (Microsoft) for beginners

Definition

Excel can be a very powerful and intimidating tool to use at the same time.

Thus, it is imperative to put up this guide to help the beginners get started.

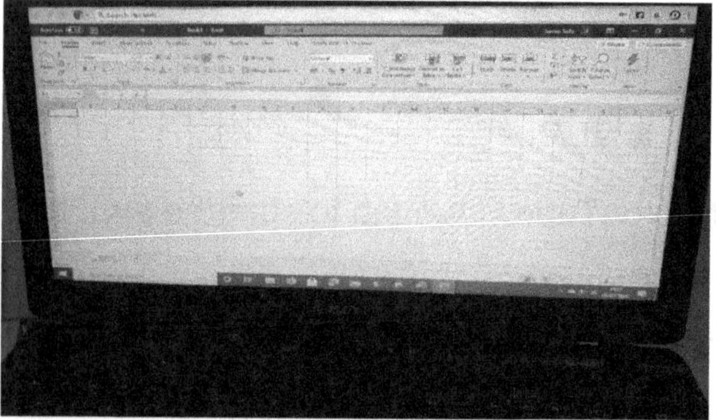

Excel screen

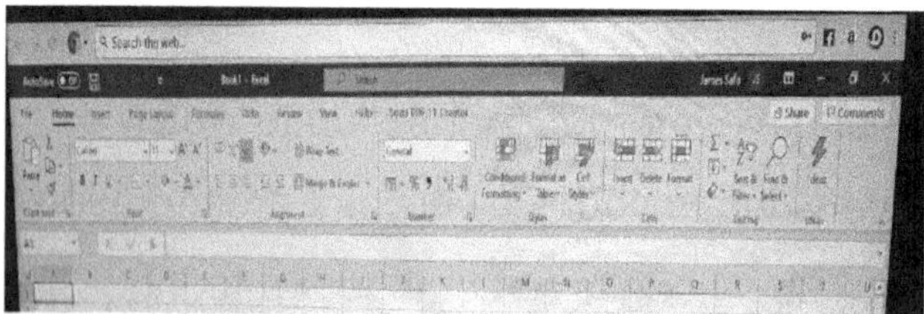

EXCEL Ribbon

1. Getting started

Select the excel from the start menu, double click the icon, look at fig. 1 below

fig. 1

When one opens excel, it looks like shown in the fig. 2 below

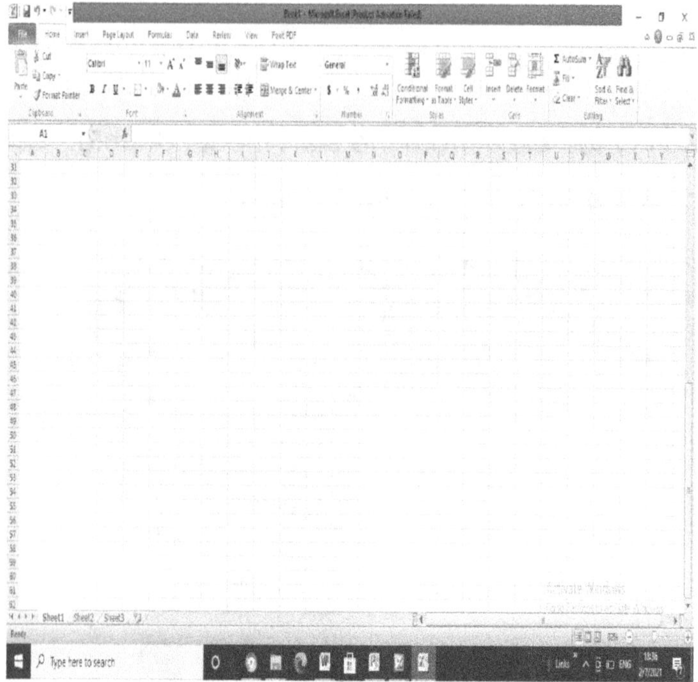

Fig. 2

To open a new spreadsheet,

click Blank workbook.

To open the already existing spreadsheet, click "open other workbooks" located in the left corners, click "browse" on the lower left side of the new window. Look at fig. 3

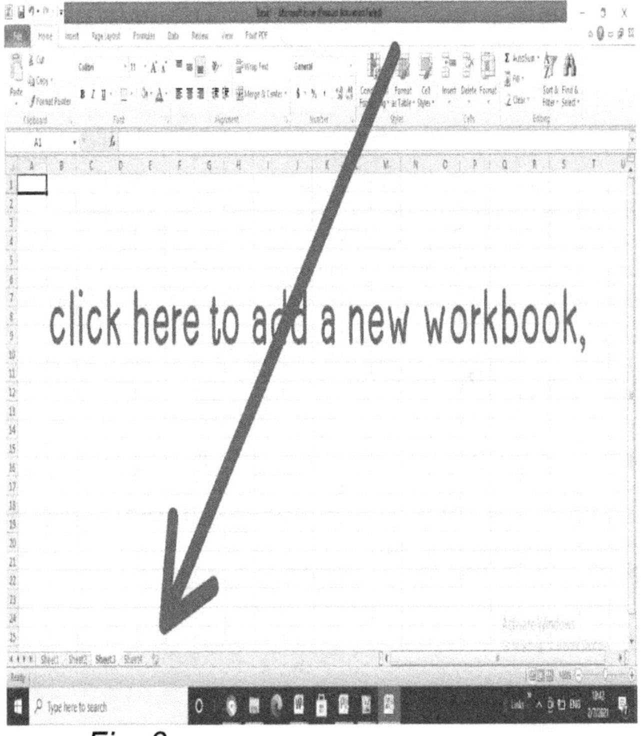

Fig. 3

Then use the file explorer to find the workbook

you're looking for,

select it,

and click Open.

Note

A workbook is different from spreadsheet in that a workbook is an excel file. It has an extension of .XLSX but in the older version of Excel, the extension is .XLS

A spreadsheet on the other hand is a single sheet inside a workbook. In one workbook, there could be several sheets. These are accessed via the tabs shown on fig. 2 above.

How to work with ribbons

Ribbon is the central control panel in the excel. Ribbon allows you to do anything you want in the excel as shown in fig. 4 below.

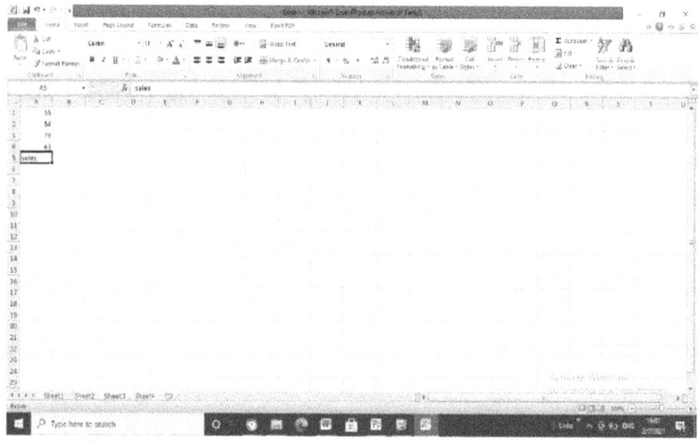

Fig. 4

Widening the column

Automatically , the width of a cell allows only eight characters of any data entry to be displayed before that data spills over into the next cell to the right. If the cell or cells to the right are blank, the entered data is displayed in the worksheet.

To widen the column:

a. Place the mouse pointer between column A and B in the column header
b. The mouse pointer changes to double-headed arrow.
c. Click the mouse, hold the left button, and drag the double-headed arrows to the right until the length of your entry is able to fit in the new size of the column.
d. Widen columns always when you need to put data that cannot fit in the normal size of the columns. As shown in fig. 5, place the cursor in the marked point at drag it.

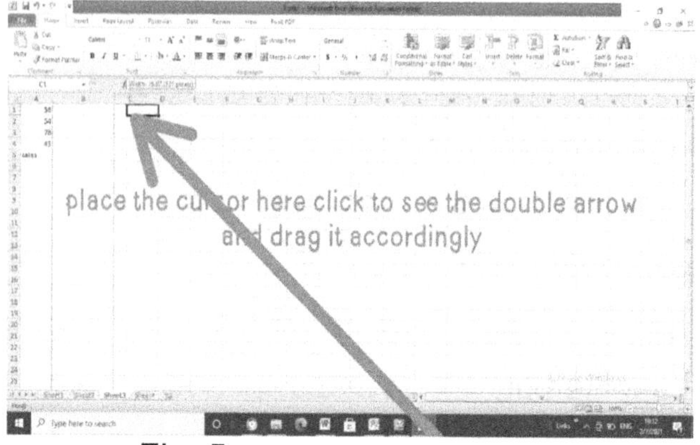

Fig. 5

Adding the date and a name range

Adding data and date is a common practice when working with spreadsheets. Date shows when lastly the sheet was updated. Date can be added in the excel in a number of ways. The ways are inbuilt with the formulas. Methods of adding date include:

The Today function- updates itself every time there are recalculations. To add the today function:

Click on the cell C2 to make it active

Click on the formulas tab in the ribbon

iii.   Click on the "date & time" option

iv.   Click on the today function to bring the formula builder

v.   Click "done"

Using pivot tables

To recognize and make sense of data

Pivot tables are used to rearrange data in a spreadsheet. The tables will not change the data but will sum up the values and compare various information in the spreadsheet. All depends on how you wish to use the data.

To create a Pivot table, go to Data> Pivot Table. Automatically, the Pivot table is populated.

You have launched the Pivot table then you have four options. These are:

a. Report filter- allows you to look at one specific row in your data set.

b. Column labels- are the headers in the dataset

c. Row labels- are rows in the dataset.

d. Value- allows you to look at the data differently instead of pulling one numerical value, you could sum, average, maximize, minimize the data.

For example, if I wanted to create a Pivot table to show different beverages, I will have the table shown in fig. 6.

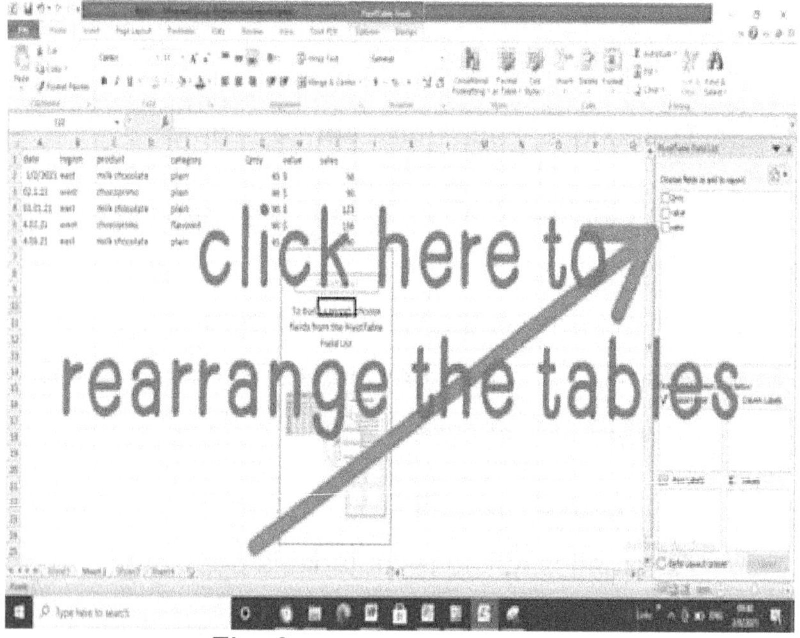

Fig. 6

The Pivot table shows the total sales of products and can be rearranged to show the sales per region, category, by month, on daily basis etc.

Adding an extra column or row

As you work around with your data, you may discover you are continually expecting to add more rows and columns. Doing this you need to highlight the number of existing columns, right-click and select "insert". Look at fig.7 below

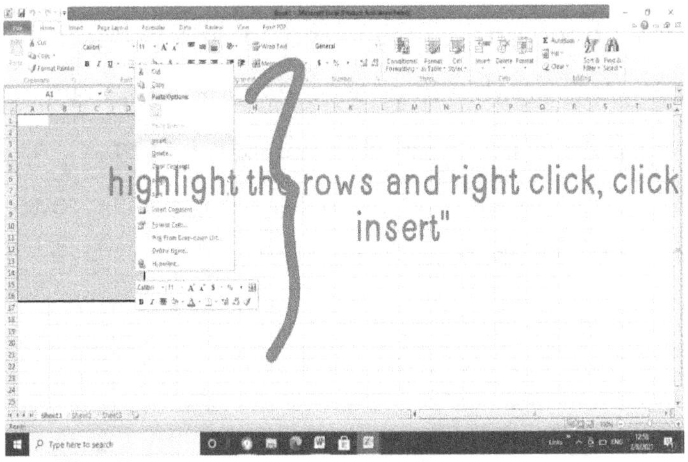

Fig. 7

Using filters to simplify the data

If you are working either a large data, you do not have to look at all the rows at the same time. You may only want to look at data that follow certain criteria. Therefore, you use filters. Filters make it easy to pare the data to view one row at a time. Filters can be added in each column; therefore, you need to choose the cell you want to view at a time.

Let us look at the example below. Add a filter by clicking the Data tab and selecting "Filter." Clicking the arrow next to the column headers and you'll be able to choose whether you want your data to be organized in ascending or descending order, as well as which specific rows you want to show as shown in fig. 8

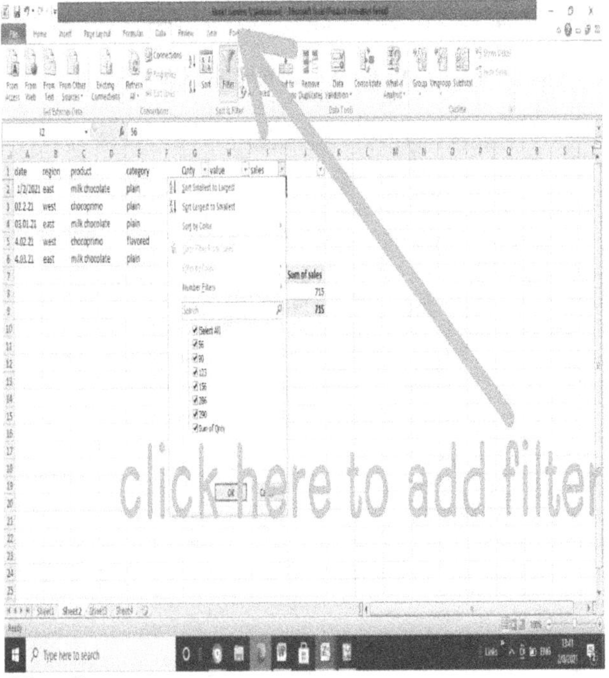

Fig. 8

To remove duplicate data points or sets

Large data set could have some duplicated sets. For instance in a list of company employees in a payroll some names could appear more than once. In such a situation, you need to remove the duplicated data.

To remove this data, highlight the row or column you want to remove the duplicate. Go to data tab, select "remove duplicate". Confirm in the pop-up "remove duplicate". Look at fig. 9

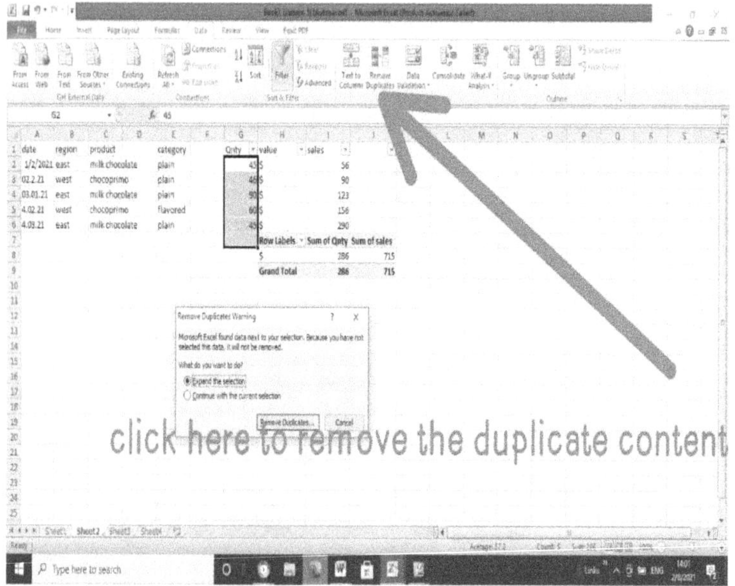

Fig. 9

Transpose rows into column

At times, you have low rows in the spreadsheet and wants to convert one row into a column or vice versa. It is quite hectic to copy paste these data one after the other. Thus, the transpose feature saves your time allowing you to move your data from a column to a row and vice versa.

Highlight the column that you want to transpose into a row. Right click it and select "copy". Select the cell on your spreadsheet you wish your new row or column to begin. Right click on that cell and select "paste special". A module will appear -- at the bottom, you will see an option to transpose. Check that box and select OK. Your column will now be transferred to a row or vice-versa as shown in fig. 10

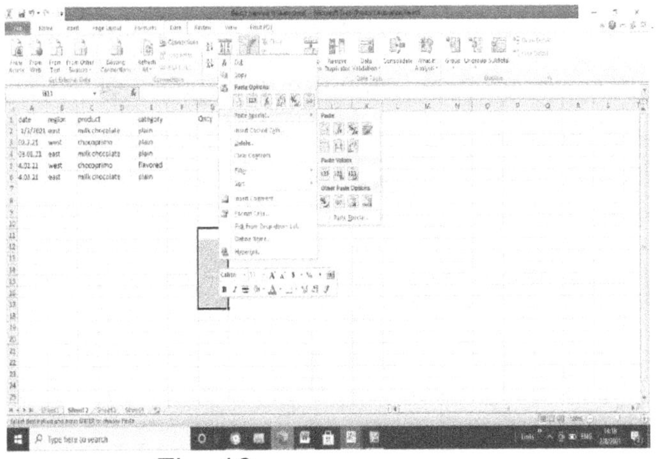

Fig. 10

Splitting information between columns

Some time you may wish to slit the information in one cell into a column. For instance, you want to separate someone's name into surname and first name.

Highlight the column you want to slit. Go to data tab, select "text to column", and select the delimited" or" fixed width. Delimited means breaking up the column based on characters such as commas, spaces, or tabs, fixed width means you want to select the exact location on all the columns that you want the split to occur. Look at fig. 11

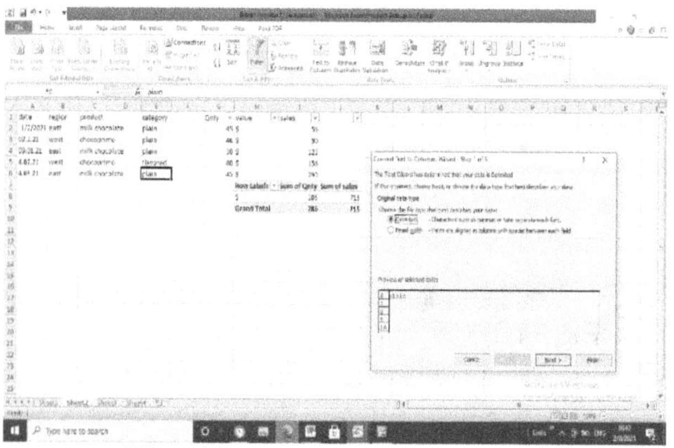

Fig. 11

Excel formulas

Excel can perform complex calculations as well as other simple calculations including adding, subtracting, multiplying and dividing. This is explained below:

To add, use the + sign, subtract use – sign, to multiply use * sign and to divide use / sign.

Get the average of numbers in your cells.

If you want the average of a set of numbers, you can use the formula =AVERAGE (Cell Range). If you want to sum up a column of numbers, you can use the formula =SUM (Cell Range).

Now you have known the basic tips about MS excel, we'll explore deeper in the next tutorials.

Chapter 8

Excel (Microsoft) Advance

synopsis

In this era, most businesses use various software to run their daily activities of the company efficiently. The software helps in timesaving, efficient use of business resources and assist in the execution of data. Microsoft Excel is the most common software use by many businesses, be it a small business, medium and large firms in managing, storing and data analysis. Microsoft excel is mostly preferred due to the unique qualities which allow the users to use the functions and formulas present in excel in solving complex calculations. Microsoft excel has advanced processes and procedures, as discussed below.

VLOOKUP

This function is also known as Hook-up and aids the user in VLOOKUP pieces of large data sets.

When this function is applied, it enables the user to pull a particular data and show the removed data in a new table formed. Thus, the user can search a value in a column and return a different value in the same row the previous value was found. Apart from many benefits of this function, the function has some limitations, including taking a long time to run, especially in large workbooks. Another limitation is that it is a must for the lookup column to be the leftmost in the data selected for calculations.

See fig. 1 below

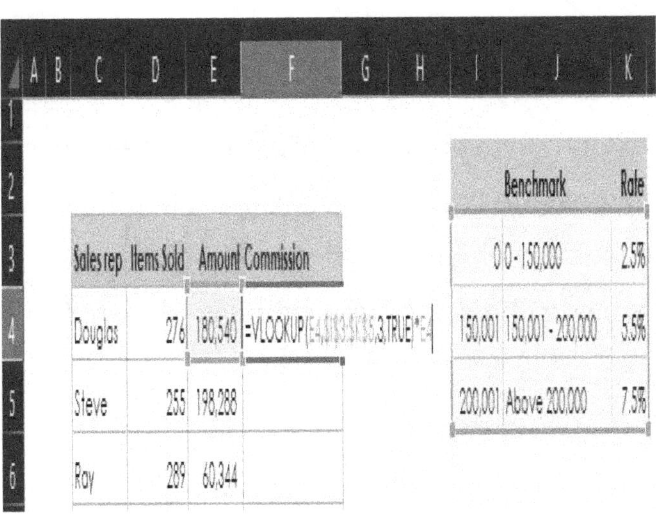

Fig.1

Index and match

When the user wants to return a value from a collection of cells depending on the previous position, the index function is the best. Where user need to check a value in a group of cells, the match function is suitable. When the index and the match functions are combined, they are used to execute a VLOOKUP and are very flexible. Combination of the two parts allows the user to search in the entire spreadsheet for any value instead of the VLOOKUP that allows search only in the leftmost column. These excel formulas help an organization since they play a significant role in financial modelling and financial analysis. The below example index and match formulas are used to return the sales part # according to the month selected. Therefore since the month and part# are variables, it is possible to change the two of them. Look at fig. 2

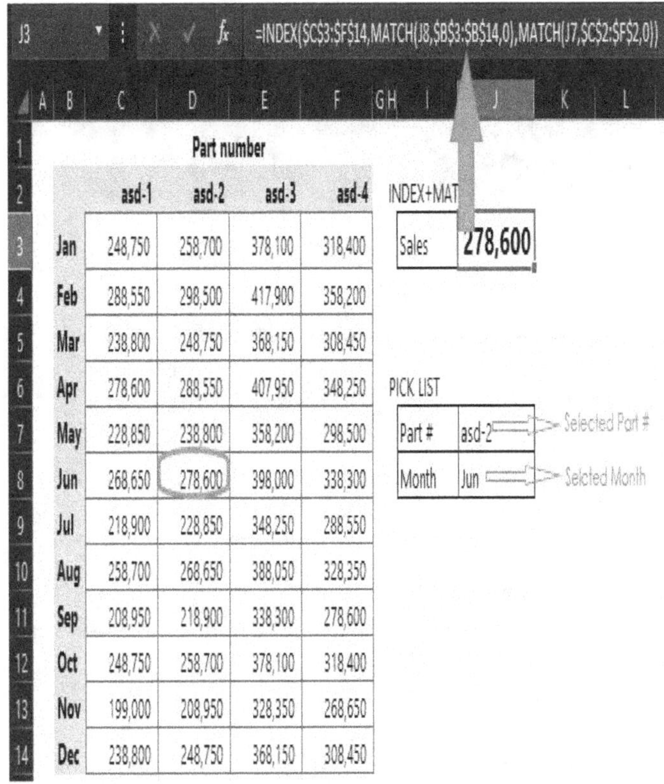

	asd-1	asd-2	asd-3	asd-4
Jan	248,750	258,700	378,100	318,400
Feb	288,550	298,500	417,900	358,200
Mar	238,800	248,750	368,150	308,450
Apr	278,600	288,550	407,950	348,250
May	228,850	238,800	358,200	298,500
Jun	268,650	278,600	398,000	338,300
Jul	218,900	228,850	348,250	288,550
Aug	258,700	268,650	388,050	328,350
Sep	208,950	218,900	338,300	278,600
Oct	248,750	258,700	378,100	318,400
Nov	199,000	208,950	328,350	268,650
Dec	238,800	248,750	368,150	308,450

Fig.2

Indirect formula

The user uses the indirect formula is returning a cell that is specified by a text string. This formula is mostly used to convert a reference previously resembled a text to be a proper reference. The indirect formula is mainly used when referring to a different sheet or another worksheet when creating a dependent drop-down list and locking a cell reference. Below is a simple illustration of

an indirect formula used in an excel workbook.
See fig. 3

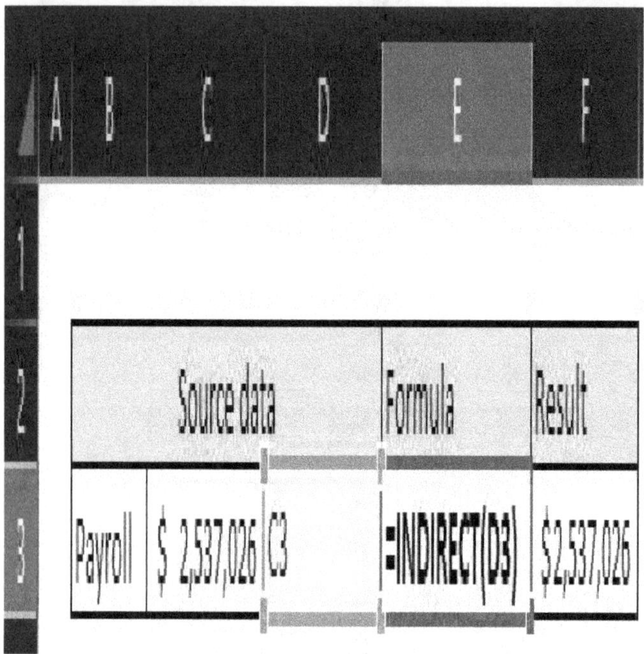

Fig.3

The Nested 'IF' Function / IFS

A foundation of logical formulas found in the
excel spreadsheet used to execute various
commands that depend on whether the sets
given are met is the IF Function. These formulas
are very long with different IF and for a human
being's mind, it is challenging to keep all the
tracks required of the logic and the comas used
in this formula.

Daily users of excel in their work are mostly using these formulas and come up with the long if function in their data execution. See fig. 4a below.

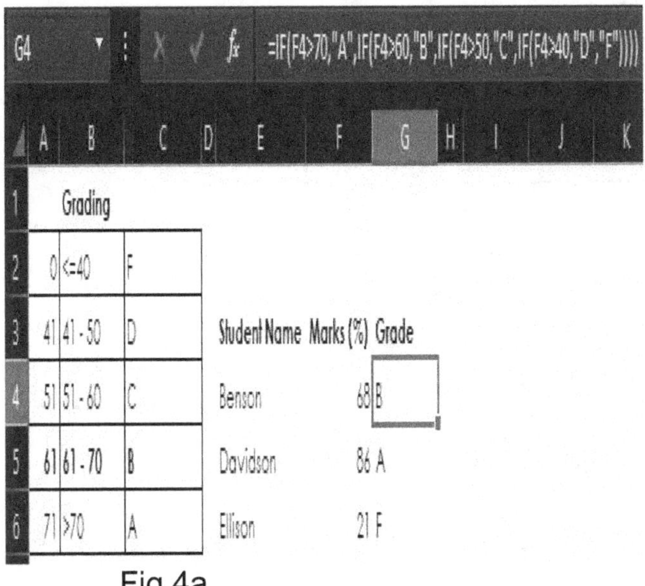

Fig.4a

As a result of introducing the IFS function, the long-nested IF is simplified and gives a similar product that is carried with a more straightforward method that is simple to read to various people. See fig. 4b below.

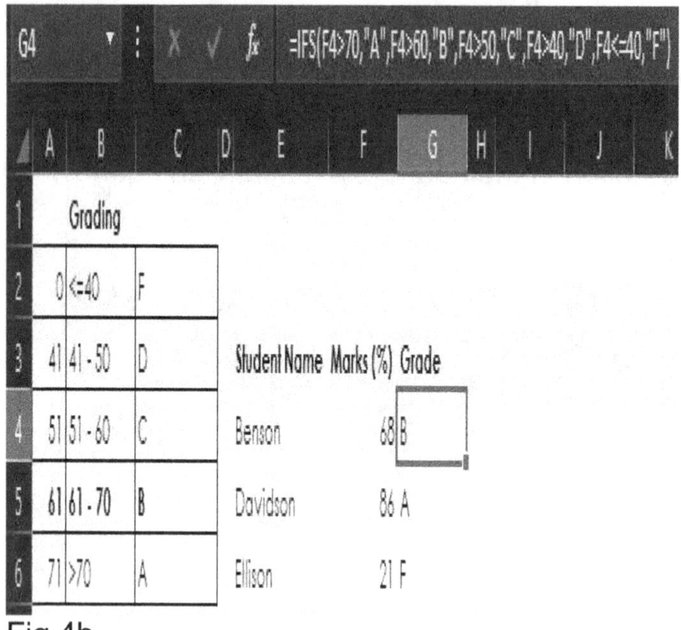

Fig.4b

The SUM IF AND SUMI FS (conditional SUM)

These formulas add up cells that are in a particular range and meeting a specific condition. There exist a difference in the two formulas where SIMIF can evaluate a single criterion only while SUMIFS evaluated multiple met states. See fig. 5

	Recruiter	Job Req. No	Start Date	Salary	FTE	Location	Salary cost for Mombasa
1	Recruiter	Job Req. No	Start Date	Salary	FTE	Location	Salary cost for Mombasa
2	James E	121212	13/02/2009	65,000	Yes	HQ	270,000
3	Richard R	212121	17/02/2009	55,000	Yes	HQ	SUMIF($F$2:$F$13,"Mombasa",$D$2:$D$13)
4	Richard R	313131	23/02/2009	65,000	Yes	HQ	
5	James E	414141	02/03/2009	75,000	Yes	HQ	
6	Jimmy G	515151	02/03/2009	85,000	Yes	Eldoret	Salary Cost for Mombasa for Non-FTEs
7	Jimmy G	616161	10/03/2009	95,000	Yes	Eldoret	130,000
8	Jimmy G	717171	12/03/2009	85,000	Yes	Eldoret	SUMIFS($D$2:$D$13,$F$2:$F$13,"Mombasa", $E$2:$E$13,"No")
9	Jackie K	818181	15/03/2009	75,000	Yes	Mombasa	
10	Okoth H	919191	24/03/2009	65,000	Yes	Mombasa	
11	Okoth H	323232	14/04/2009	40,000	No	Mombasa	
12	Okoth H	424242	15/04/2009	40,000	No	Mombasa	
13	Jackie K	525252	16/04/2009	50,000	No	Mombasa	

Fig.5

SUMPRODUCT

The subproducts also known as the arrays, they are noted as array1, array2 to array. These subproducts are part of the advanced functions in Microsoft Excel and used to handle the collections.

The subproducts are mostly applied by multiplying the components, and after the multiplication, the sum of products will be the final answer.

This is a fundamental technique in data analysis. This function has various uses; they can count the number of arrays, and the arrays include the COUNTIFS and the SUMIFS. The good part about using the subproducts to calculate this SUMIFS and the COUNTIFS is that it brings flexibility in the functions. I have tried to show how the subproducts can be used by the example below. The standards establish the computation of the average in the business selling price of all their products and then use the subproducts to get the selling price and quantity. It is divided by total sales. This subproducts method will be a useful method for calculating the price points, margins, and average returns. Look at fig. 6

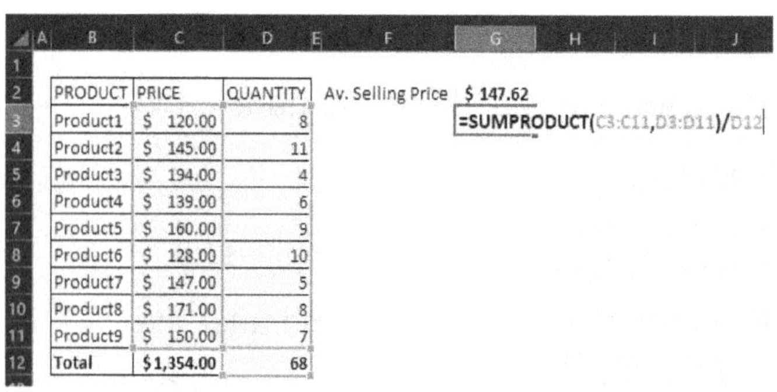

	PRODUCT	PRICE	QUANTITY	Av. Selling Price	$ 147.62
				=SUMPRODUCT(C3:C11,D3:D11)/D12	
	Product1	$ 120.00	8		
	Product2	$ 145.00	11		
	Product3	$ 194.00	4		
	Product4	$ 139.00	6		
	Product5	$ 160.00	9		
	Product6	$ 128.00	10		
	Product7	$ 147.00	5		
	Product8	$ 171.00	8		
	Product9	$ 150.00	7		
	Total	$1,354.00	68		

Fig. 6

The Choose function.

The CHOOSE function is rated as one function that so underutilized. This function is very powerful, and on the other hand, very easy to use and very easy to understand. The CHOOSE function can make the users select values ranging from one up to two hundred and fifty-four. The choice of values will always be based on the index numbers of the data. The function is more useful in financial modelling, especially when talking about scenario analysis. The CHOOSE will be more valuable than INDIRECT when selecting values from different sheets that have differences. Take an example in the case where you have three different assumptions about the revenue growth of the next year; these are 14%, 17% and 22%. By applying the CHOOSE functions its possible for one to return to 17% if you command the excel that you need the choice see fig 7 below.

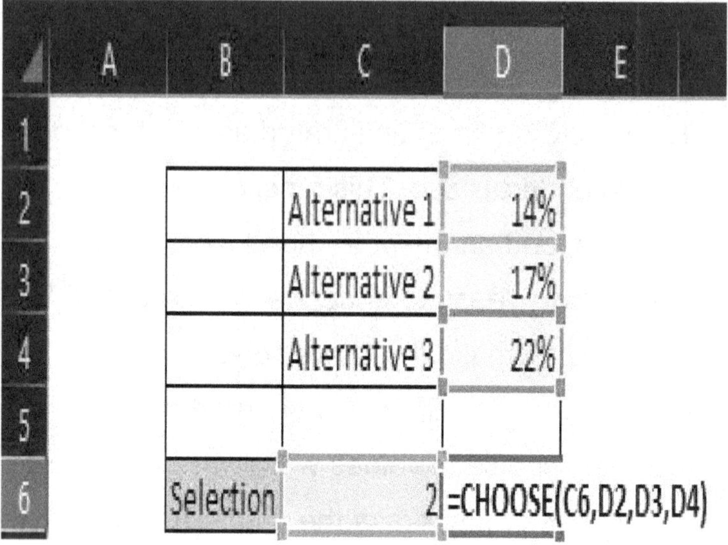

Fig.7

RIGHT, MID and LEFT.

These functions are significantly used like filters to remove texts that are not important and be left with the critical part that the writer is greatly interested in. According to Stephen Quatrini, the formula is used to show a selected number of character in a text. The RIGHT function will be used to indicate the number of characters that are on the right side of the text string, the MID function, on the other hand, will lead the characters that will appear in the middle of the series. In contrast, the LEFT part will be used to show the characters that appear on the left side of the text thread. It's easy to command the MID and show it where you want your text string to start, and it will show some characters that appear on the RIGHT of series, middle and others that appear on the left. I will give the examples to show how to use the three functions; the Right function will automatically extract the characters in the rightmost of the text strings. . See fig. 8a

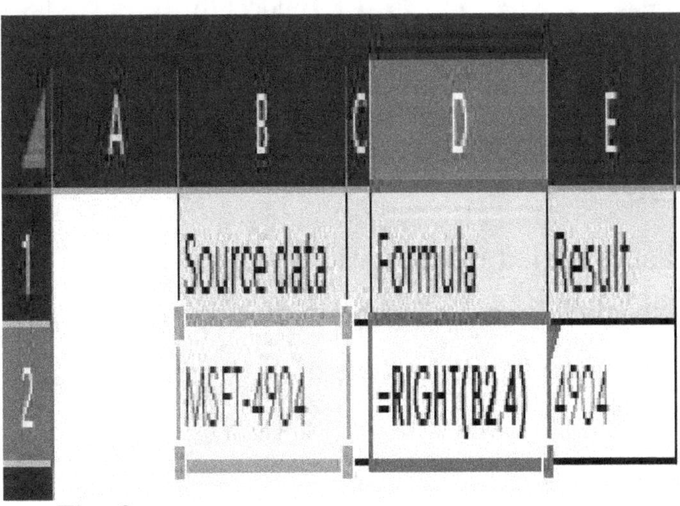

	A	Source data	Formula	Result
1		Source data	Formula	Result
2		MSFT-4904	=RIGHT(B2,4)	4904

Fig. 8a

On the other hand, the MID function will show two characters in the middle of the string. See fig. 8b below.

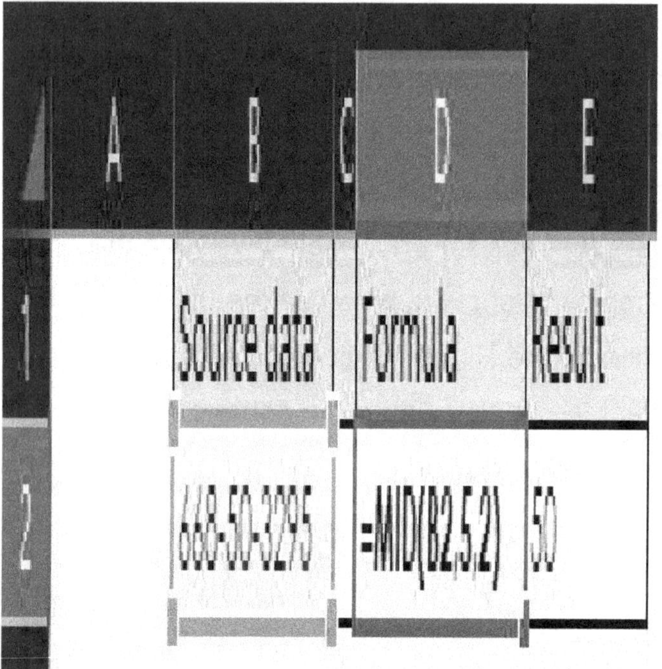

Fig.8b

Lastly, the left function will show the most extreme leftmost characters on the chosen string. See fig. 8c below

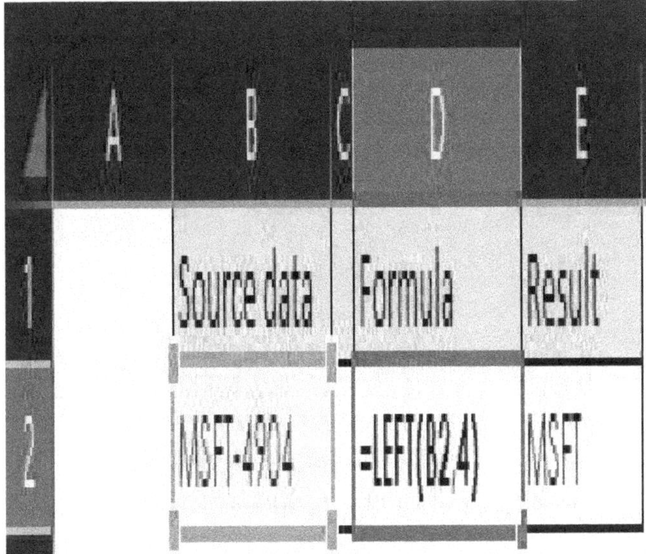

Fig. 8c

The above functions will be so essential in data analysis. It's also a very underutilized and a powerful function.

Navigation pane appears

E Navigate to Excel data source

 (E.g. Customer List)

 F double-click Customer List

 (Your data source

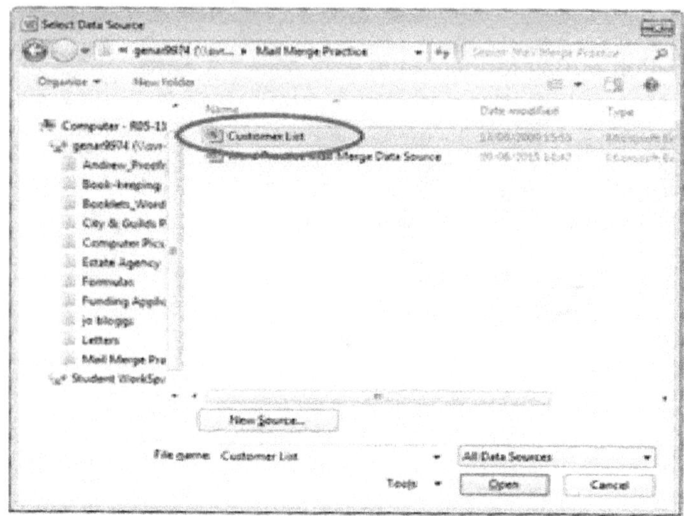

The Excel data source appears as below.

G Click on Sheet 1 to highlight it (or required sheet)

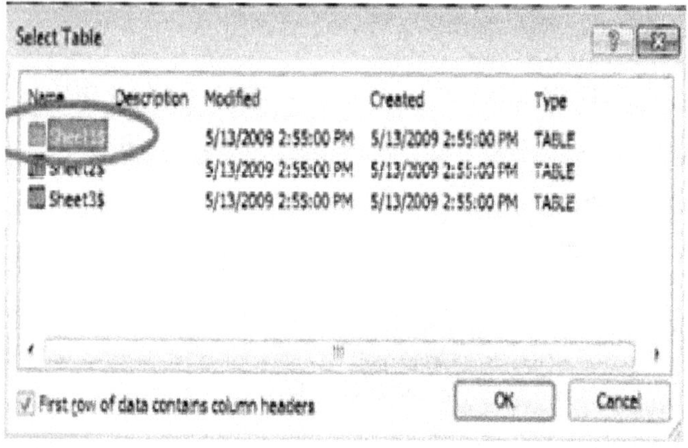

H Click Ok

Data manipulation

The data base on sheet 1 now appears as below.

You can now add or change data before the mail merge

checkboxes to add or

■		SURNAME	» | FIRST NAME	■rj TITLE ,	•ADDRESS 1 *
Customer list.xls	F	Keyworth	Rita	Mrs	6 Dale View
Customer Listels	F	Cox	May	Mrs	i Main Street
Customer Listxls	F	Tafari	Margaret	Mrs	22 Pippin Grove
Customer Ustjds	F	Waterfall	Kim	Miss	3 Carrington Place
Customer List.xls	F	Appleyard	Clare	Miss	57 Kensington Read
Customer List-xls	F	Sing	Mandy	Mrs	38 Blossom Court
Customer Listels	F	Stevens	Julie	Mrs	92 Vickory Drive
-1		m			»

I Click **Ok**

Merge field names appear

L Double-click, on the page, where you

want a field name to

be inserted

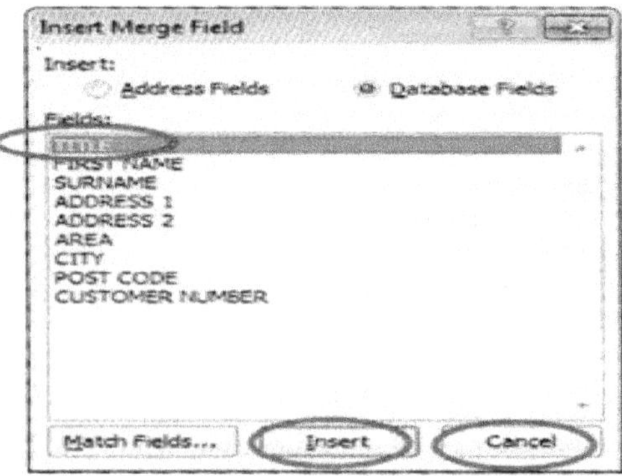

Click Insert

or Click *Cancel*

Click Next:

Preview your letters

Mail Merge

Write your letter

If you have not already done so,
 write your letter now

To add recipient information to your letter,
 dick a location in the document,
and then dick one of the items below.
 Address block...
Greeting line...
Electronic postage...
m More items...
When you have finished writing your letter,
 dick Next.
Then you can preview
and personalize each recipient's letter.

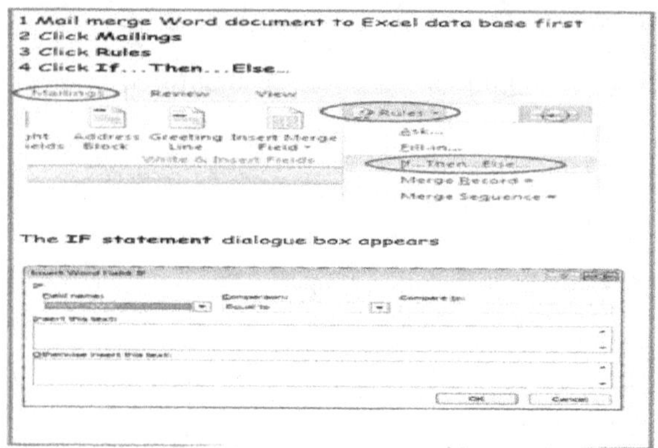

5. Make all your selections and written statements within the dialogue box:

A)   Field name: Select column header

B)   Comparison: Select "Greater than or equal"

C)   Compare to: Type "8"

D)   Insert this text: Type your first message

E)   Otherwise insert this text: Type your alternative

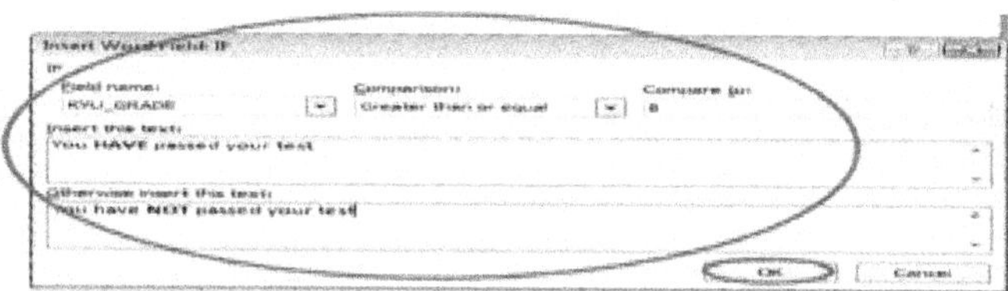

6) Click **OK**

Chapter 9

Access (Microsoft) for Beginners

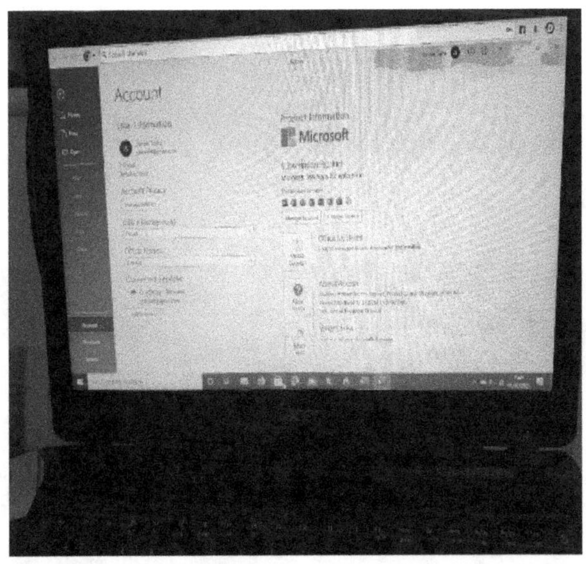

a. How to start the Microsoft access

Mostly, Microsoft access comes bundled with the Microsoft office. Two ways can be used to launch the application.

From the windows "start" button. Look at fig. 12

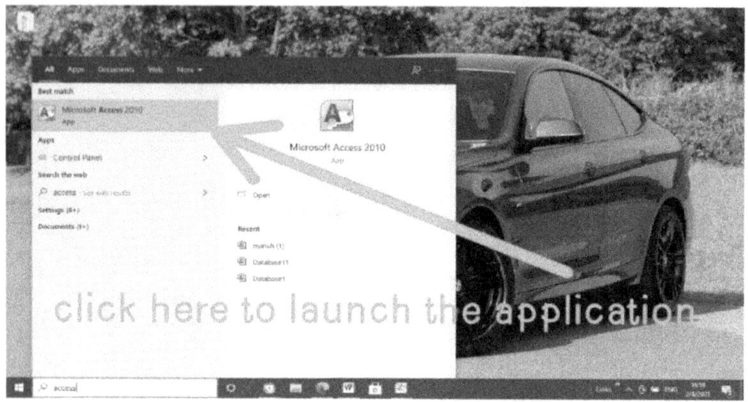

Fig. 12

From the desktop, right click> 'new' option. Look at fig. 13

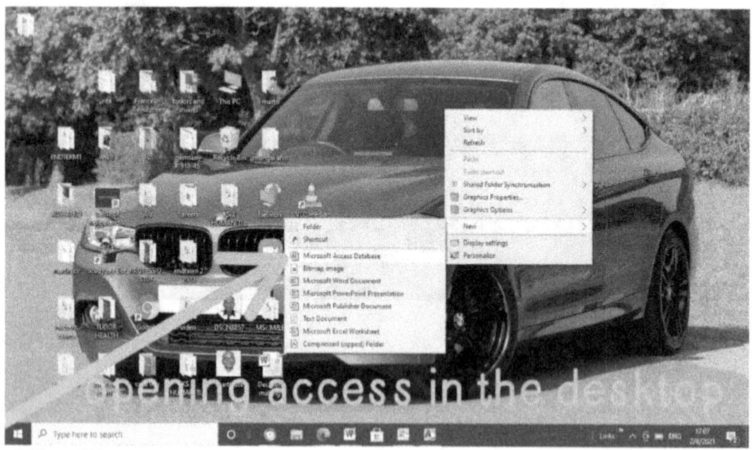

Fig 13

Microsoft access will appear like shown in fig. 14 below

Fig. 14

Creating a database

To get started click "create" below the blank database.

Database in reference to MS access include bookcase where books are stored and i-pods where there are collections of music and other items. Generally, MS access is your home for all the tables, forms, reports, queries among others.

Access stores data in an organized manner for easier access and retrieval. Look at fig. 15 below.

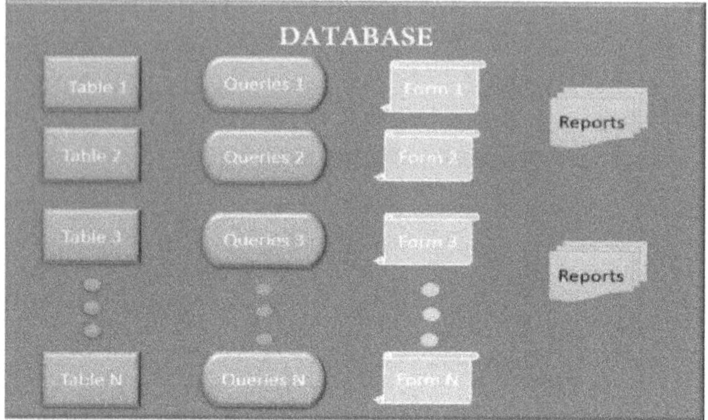

Fig. 15

Two ways are used in creating a database

a. Creating database from a template
b. Creating a blank database.

Creating a database from a template

There are many situations where we need to start with some readymade database template for given requirements.

MS Access provides many ready to use templates for such types of databases requirements where the data structure is already defined.

You can keep customizing the template structure further as per our requirement.

MS Access Databases example includes Contacts, Student, Time tracking, etc

To create database from the template,

Open "file" on the MS access application. You will get the page as shown fig. 16 below

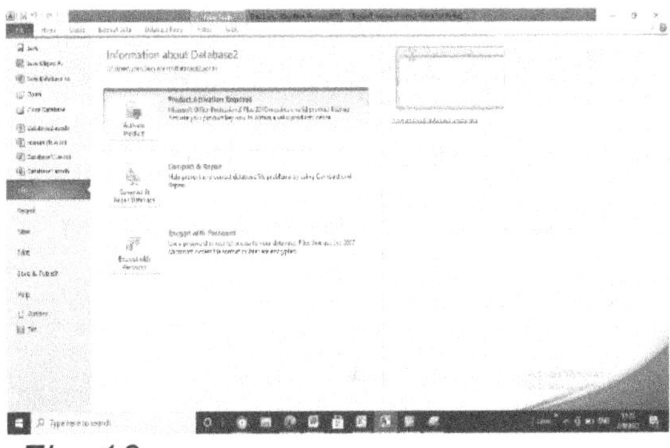

Fig. 16

Figure 17 below is a display of the templates upon clicking "new"

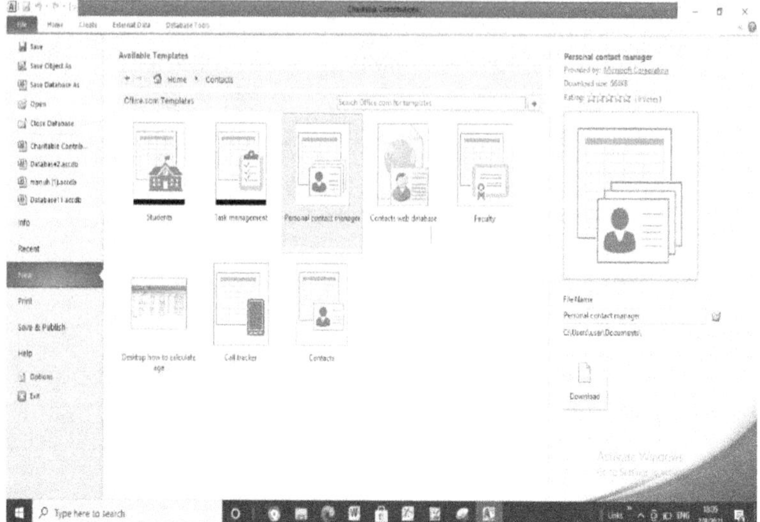

Fig. 17

Select any template by clicking on it, for instance, select "contact template", here is the results in fig. 18:

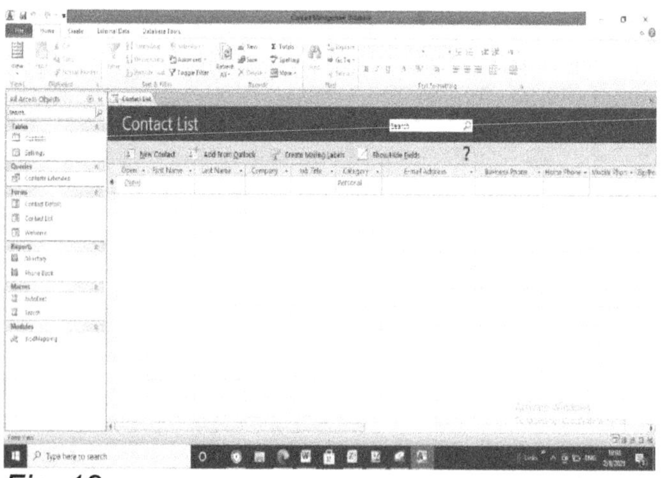

Fig. 18

You can click on any of the objects from left navigation pane and open that object for further references and work. For instance, click "contact details" a different form comes up, it appears as shown in fig. 19.

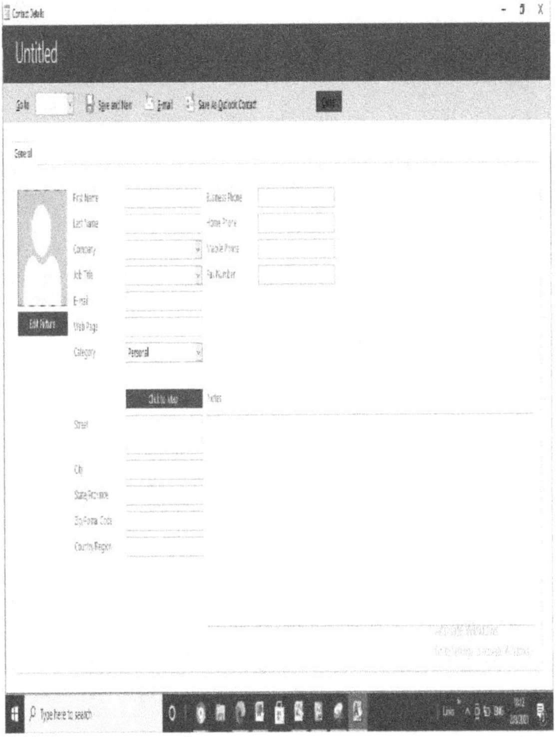

Fig. 19

c. Creating a blank database

1. In the MS access, click on the file>new. The new appearance is shown in fig. 20 and 21 below:

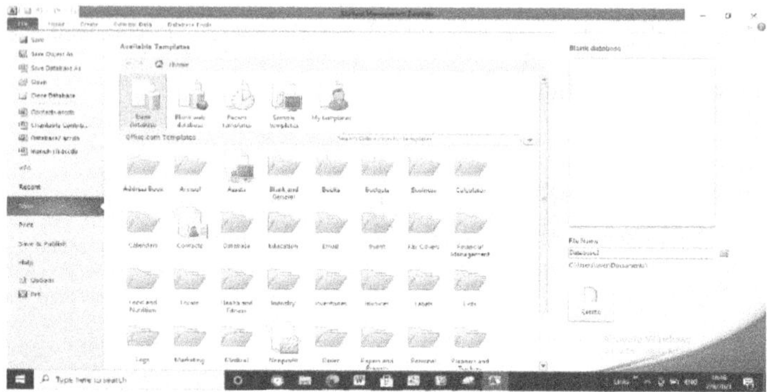

Fig. 20

2. Click on the blank database

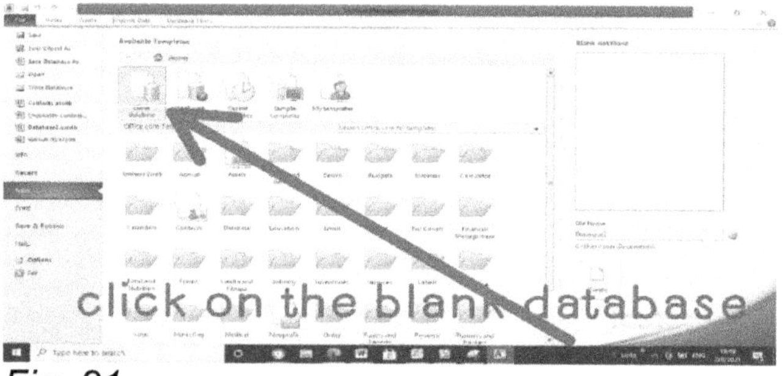

Fig. 21

How to create tables

First aim of MS excel is to store data. Therefore, tables are essential parts of the MS excel. After creation of tables, row and columns must be inserted. Tables in MS excel are created in two ways:

1. Created from 'design view" as shown in fig. 22

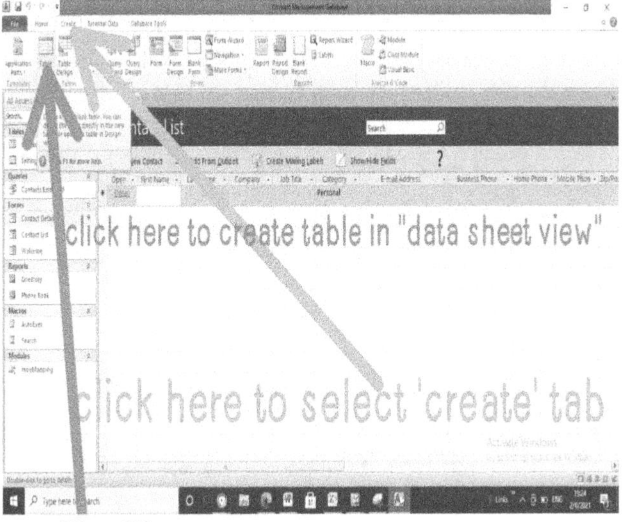

Fig. 22

2. The system displays a default table labeled "Table 1" as shown in fig. 23

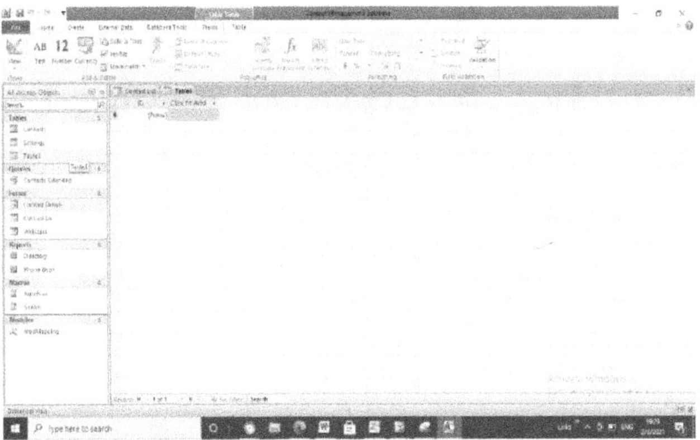

Fig. 23

rename the table

To rename the table, double click the column
header and write the new name. Look at
fig. 24

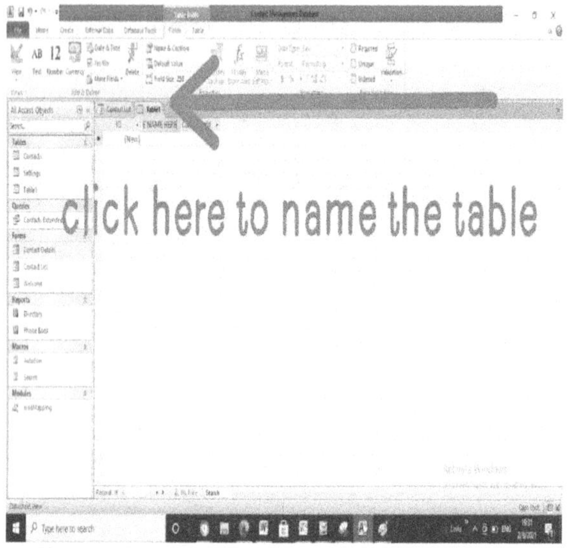

Fig. 24

Creating table design

Step 1) First Click Create tab. Then from Tables
group, click Table.   look at fig. 25 below

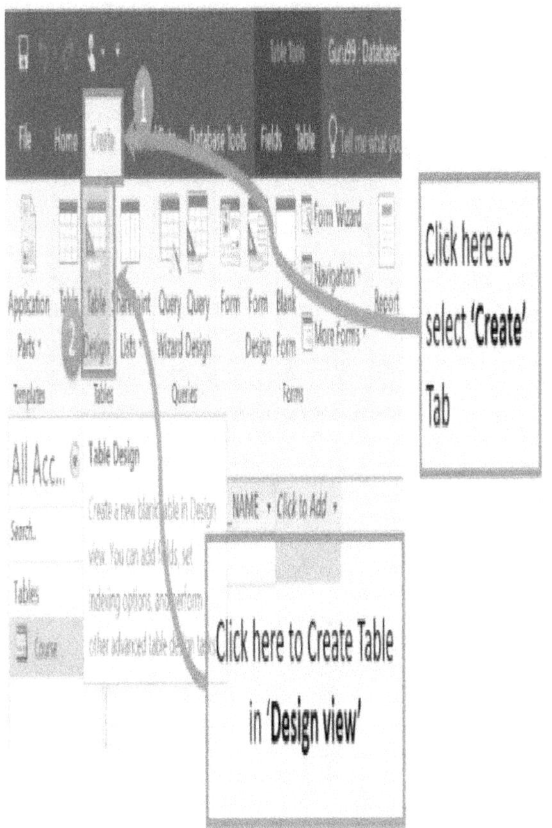

Fig. 25

Step 2)

 Table Dialog box appears. For each Field
enter Filed Name, Data Type and Description.
Look at fig. 26

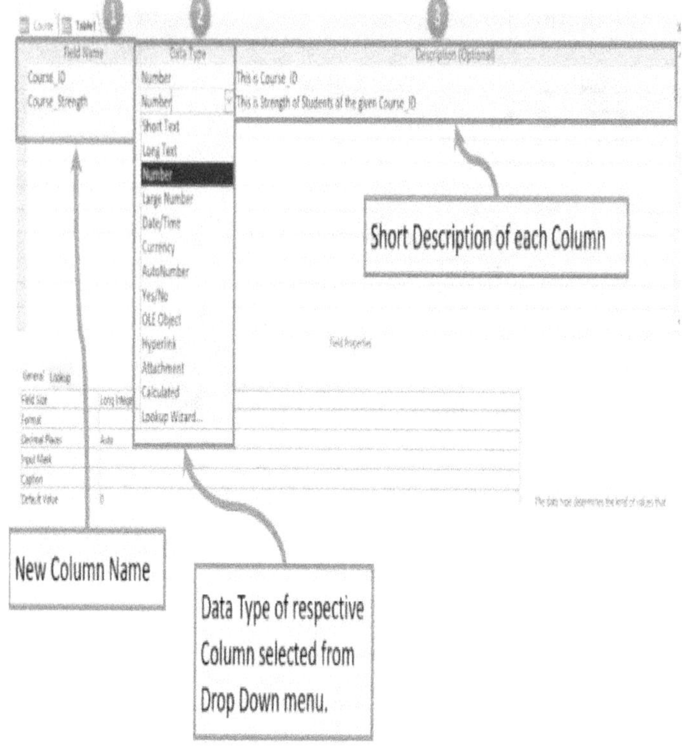

Fig. 26

Steps 3)

To Add Course_ID as Primary Key

select it and Click on 'Primary Key.' Coursed will be Preceded by KEY ICON as shown below:

Adding data

Select Views> datasheet view option in the ribbon and add some data. Look at fig. 27

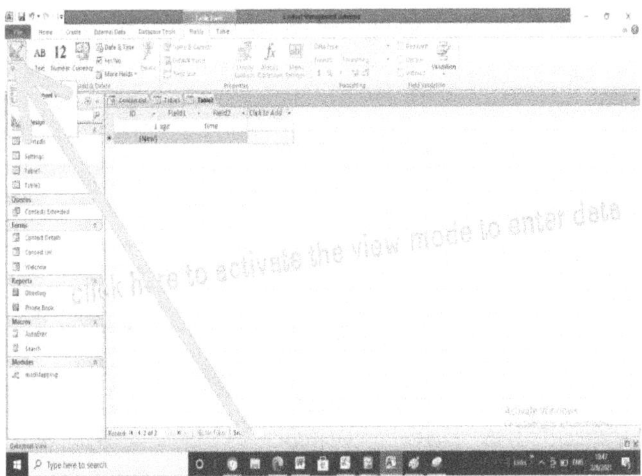

Fig. 27

It is easy to enter data in a datasheet and update it accordingly. If you want to delete some data, select the entire row or column as shown in fig. 28 below

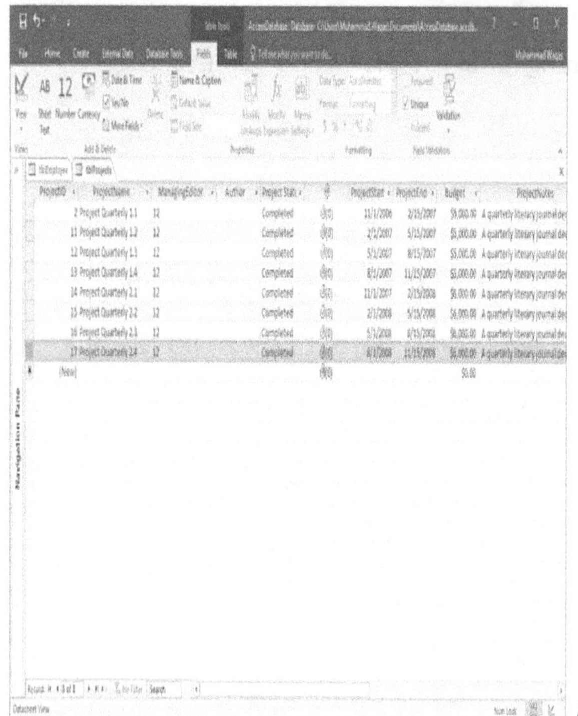

Fig. 28

Now press the delete button. The popup will display the confirmation message as shown in fig.29

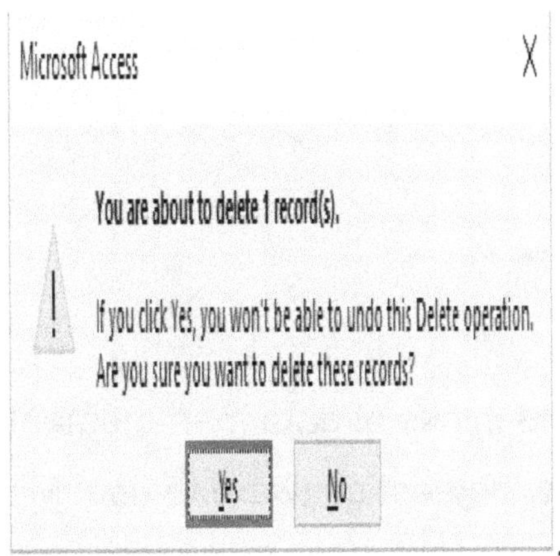

Fig 29

Now you have known the basic tips about MS access, we'll explore deeper in Access

Chapter 10
Access (Microsoft) Advance

When one thinks of data management, Microsoft access is the best software to use. Microsoft Access is a powerful software used by most people and mostly those with big organizations and businesses in managing their data. For companies that want to create browser-based databank requests, which help run the business, Microsoft access is an easy to use tool for this purpose. When it comes to data storage, the saved data is stored automatically in a much secure way than other data storage methods and enables an easy way of sharing applications with other colleagues. Apart from data management and data keeping, Microsoft access also allows the creation of custom web applications, manages inventory, and easily tracks the organization's assets and contacts. The advanced use of Microsoft access creates tables using this software, linking the tables together, writing an SQL statement, displaying the result in an access Form, and applying conditional formatting.

Table creation

In table creation using Microsoft access, one first clicks the create tab, followed by clicking tables from the table group. The table should have a format of a short text in the company field, a threshold field to use currency format, the stock symbol field most concise format is preferred, and the include field the Yes or No design is suitable. This is the format that is suitable for a stock control table, as illustrated below in fig. 1a.

ID	Company	Stock Symbol	Include	Threshold	Click to Add
1	Company A	AAA	☑	$160.00	
2	Company B	BBB	☑	$80.00	
3	Company C	CCC	☑	$1,000.00	
4	Company D	DDD	☑	$980.00	
5	Company E	EEE	☑	$200.00	
6	Company F	FFF	☐	$150.00	

Fig. 1a

When creating stock and the stock's daily prices, a prices table is suitable where the stock prices are included in this table. The columns or fields of a price table should have the format where a daily stock price has a currency format, the company field to have a short Text format, and the stock control having a short text format.

Look at fig.1b

ID	Company	Stock Symbol	Daily Stock Price	Click to Add
1	Company A	AAA	$165.00	
2	Company B	BBB	$78.00	
3	Company C	CCC	$1,000.00	
4	Company D	DDD	$985.00	
5	Company E	EEE	$197.00	
6	Company F	FFF	$140.00	

Fig.1b

Linking the stocks and prices tables together

In combining the two tables, the first step is going to create a tab. After the create charge, the next step is to press query design on the create tab. below is an illustration of the create tab and the query design, see fig. 2a.

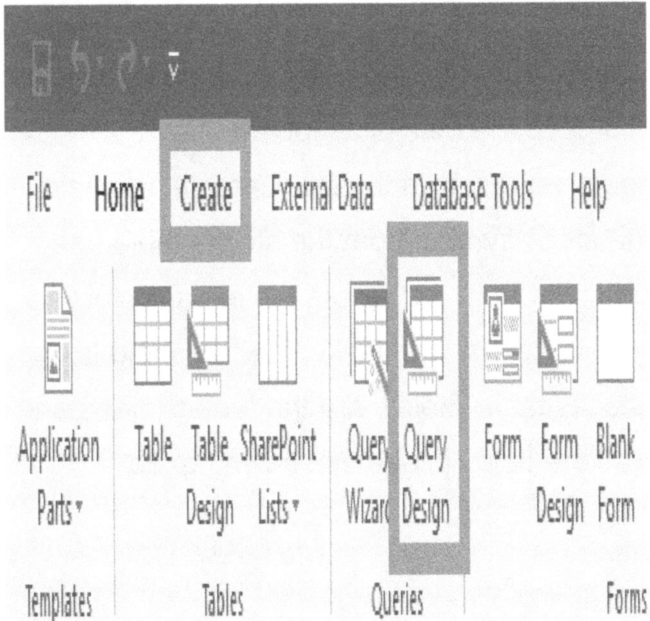

Fig.2a

After creating and query design, the stocks and the prices tables are added in the query design followed by linking the tables together using the stock control field as illustrated in fig. 2b below.

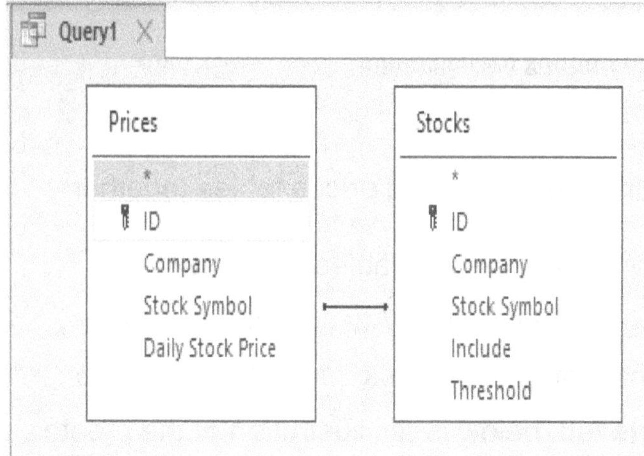

Fig.2b

In the fields name in both tables, double click on the characters and then add the fields. The fields should have the details as follows: the company's area from the stocks table, the field for the stock symbol from the stocks table, the include field from the stocks table, daily stock from prices table, and lastly, the threshold from the stocks table. Below are the tables joined and then all the fields joined as shown fig. 2c.

Field:	Company	Stock Symbol	Include	Daily Stock Price	Threshold
Table:	Stocks	Stocks	Stocks	Prices	Stocks
Sort:					
Show:	☑	☑	☑	☑	☑
Criteria:					
or:					

Fig. 2c

Writing the SQL Syntax.

After taking your time to join the price tables and the stock tables, it becomes essential to work on the SQL questions. you should change the view from the datasheet view and switch it to the SQL view. See fig. 3a

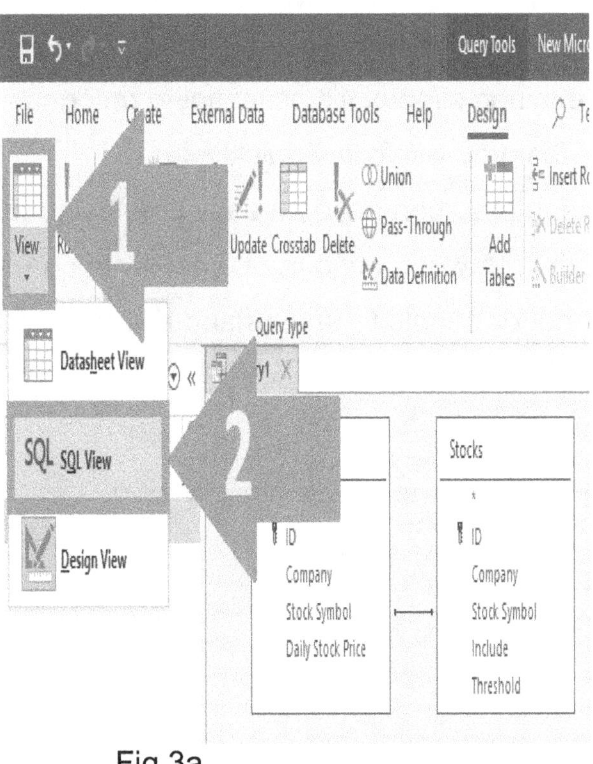

Fig.3a

After you have changed your view to SQL view, you will be able to see the SQL below, and that will mean the success of your switching views. Look at fig. 3b

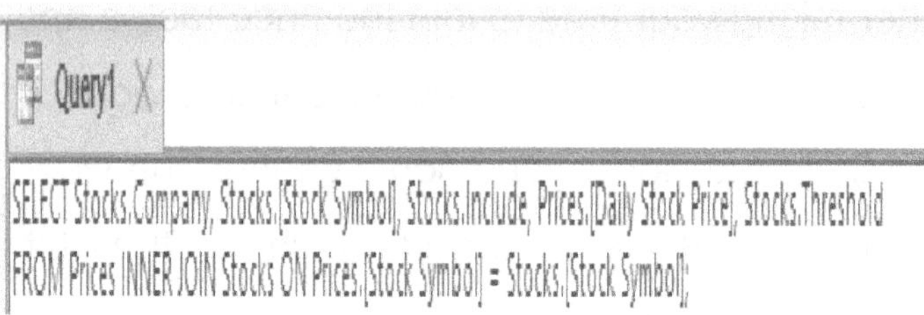

Fig.3b

To make things simple, it's essential to recognize them so that you will follow quickly, and someone tutored can have an easy time trying to learn from your work. I find the below syntax a simple one for people to understand and follow. See fig. 3c

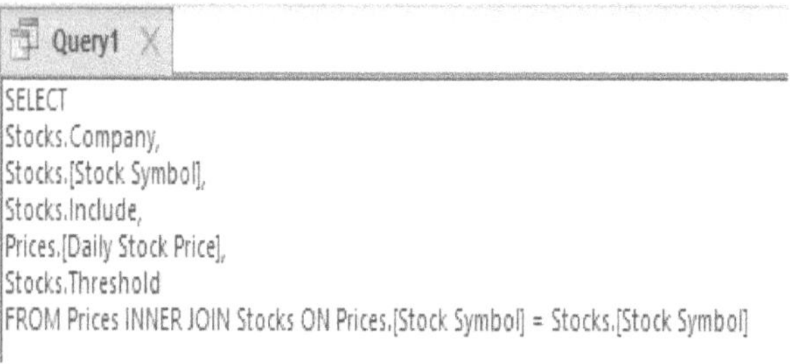

fig. 3c

After this, it's essential to add some syntax text to your view. They will make things more clear for your work. The highlighted in green below will show the added syntax. Look at fig. 3d

Fig.3d

For good references,

For good references, please take a look at the image below. It shows a complete query of the syntax. See fig. 3e

per the above illustration, there are three parts to the query; the comma added after the field of the

```
SELECT

Stocks.Company,

Stocks.[Stock Symbol],

Stocks.Include,

Prices.[Daily Stock Price],

Stocks.Threshold,


IIF(Prices.[Daily Stock Price] > Stocks.Threshold, "SELL", "KEEP") AS FLAG


FROM Prices INNER JOIN Stocks ON Prices.[Stock Symbol] = Stocks.[Stock Symbol]


WHERE Stocks.Include = YES
```

Fig.3e

threshold. The comma is to show that the syntax is continuing. Secondly, there the IIF function. This part gives the MS access to the condition that if their excess daily stock goes out of the threshold, Microsoft access should put a flag to sell. If not so the Microsoft access will remain with the flag to keep. The last part is a condition, but this a restrictive condition that will show only when the stock has been checked and approved to include and done the inclusion on the field. After the third query then you press run. Look at fig. 3f

Company	Stock Symbol	Include	Daily Stock Price	Threshold	FLAG
Company A	AAA	✓	$165.00	$160.00	SELL
Company B	BBB	✓	$78.00	$80.00	KEEP
Company C	CCC	✓	$1,000.00	$1,000.00	KEEP
Company D	DDD	✓	$985.00	$980.00	SELL
Company E	EEE	✓	$197.00	$200.00	KEEP

Fig.3f

You will notice that it's working as we wanted. The outcomes are as predict, and as per the above fig.3e, any stock that is excess of the threshold we put them as a sell. All the other daily stocks that are below the threshold point will be flagged as supposed to keep. Secondly, the stocks that have been checked and supposed to be included- on the include field- have been included. In our example, the stock from company f is not displayed because we did not check it. The query should be saved as tracking finally.

Results display using access form.

In this section, we will go a notch higher to create an access form that will enable us to maintain the information that we had got from the illustration above that includes the threshold, the stock price, and the stock that you would want to include. The information is maintained under the price tables and the stock tables. This will also help to be in a position that we can track our query. For a start, you press on the create tab, after which you will be required to click on the tab labelled as form design, and this will take you to start a new form.
See fig. 4a.

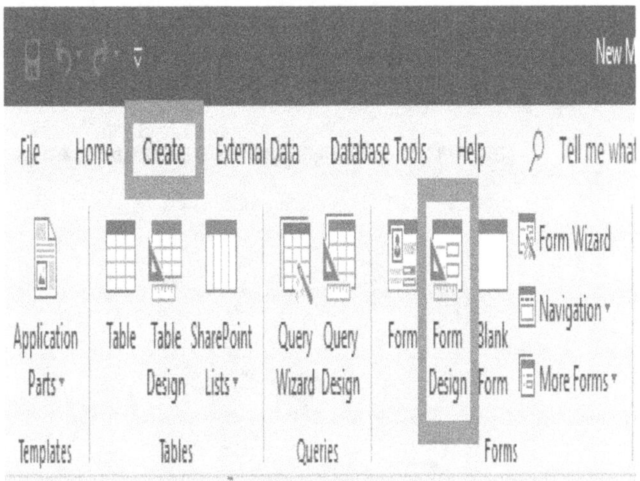

Fig.4a

Changing the background color,

Changing the background color, then it's allowed, and you are supposed to click on the Format tab, after which you can choose your preferred colours and make sure you make your choice in the shape fill. In the case below, I decide to use dark grey color for our forms. Look

at fig. 4b

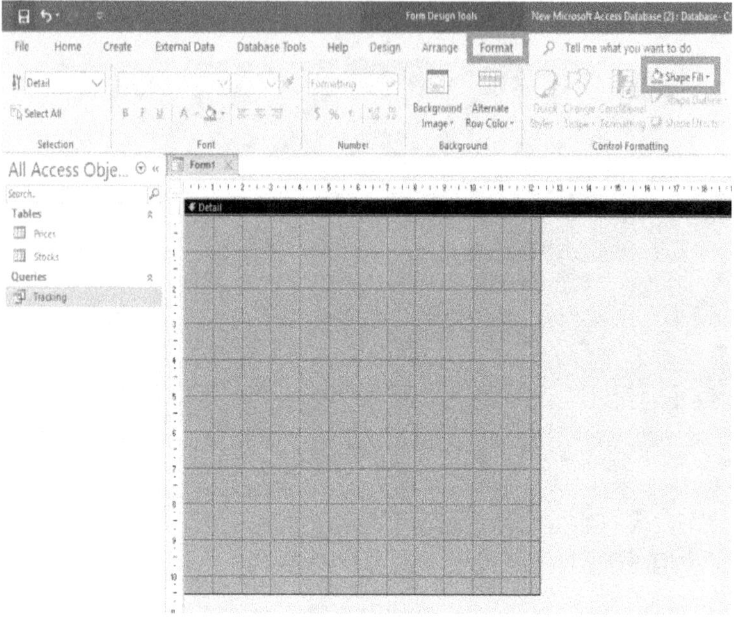

Fig.4b

To add the stock's values

you should go to the design tab, click it and then

choose the sub form/sub

report option from the panels. See fig. 4c

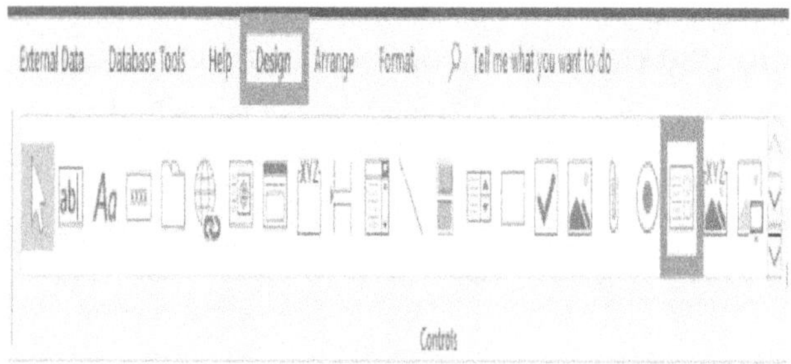

Fig.4c

The sub form should be placed as a primary form, and this will pop up a dialog box where you are supposed to click on the next. Look at fig. 4d

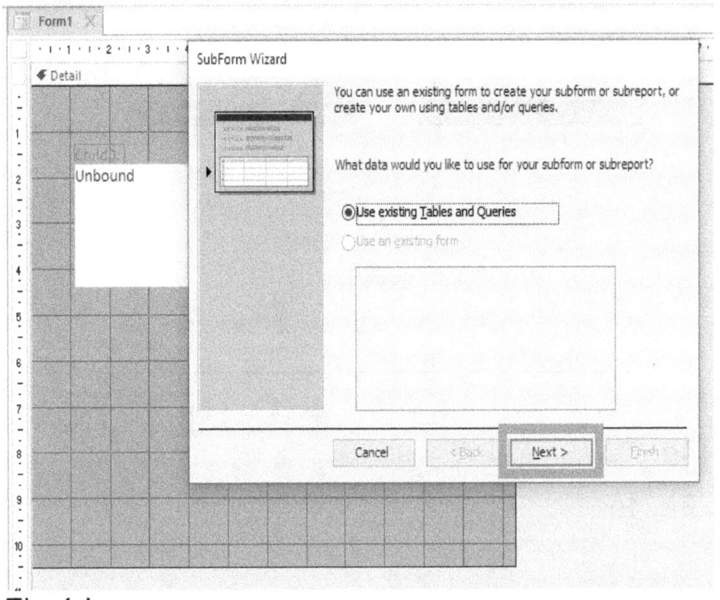

Fig.4d

Now it's is time to add the stocks table. To perform the addition, you should choose the 'tables; stock' option, which is found under the queries section on the drop-down list. After this, you will select the field; stock symbol, company, threshold, and include. Then press next. See fig.

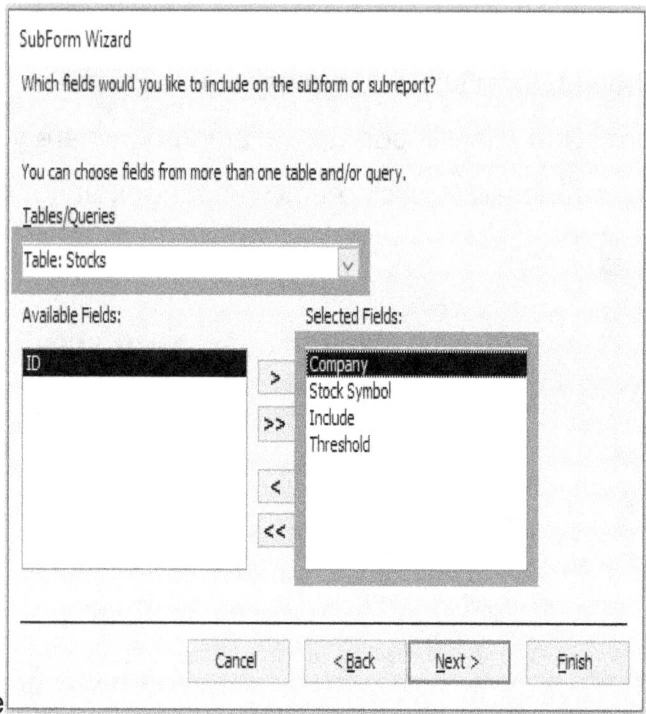

4e

Fig.4e

You will be enabled to name your sub forms, and you will call them the stock sub forms and click on finish. See fig. 4f

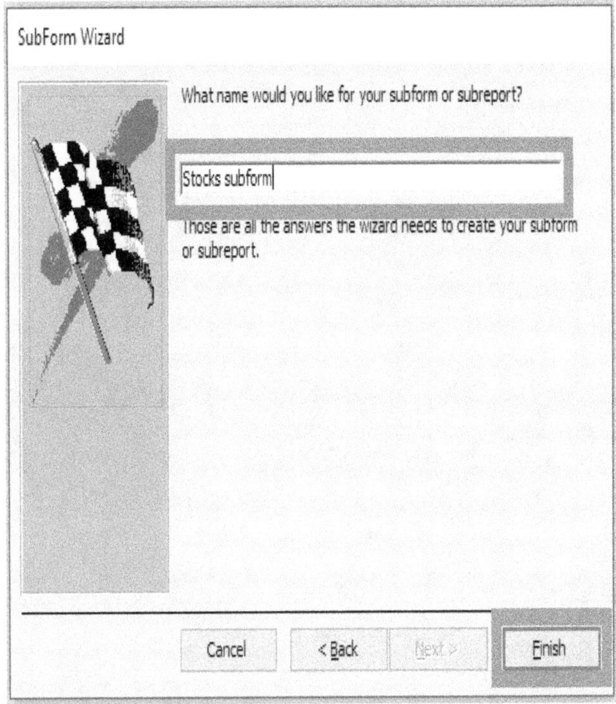

Fig.4f

Below is an image of how it will look like after pressing on the finish tab. Look at fig. 4g

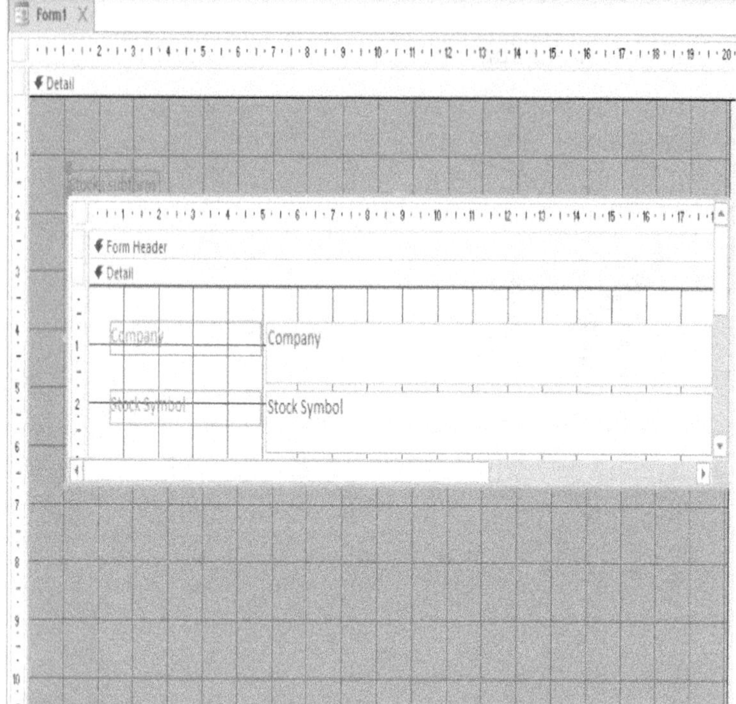

Fig.4g

Now you should your MS access to the layout view. Under this, you can prefer to use the mouse, which enables you to size and chooses your choice location. Fig 4h below shows how to change view to layout view, and the figure 4i will show how the tables will look after sizing. See fig. 4h and 4i.

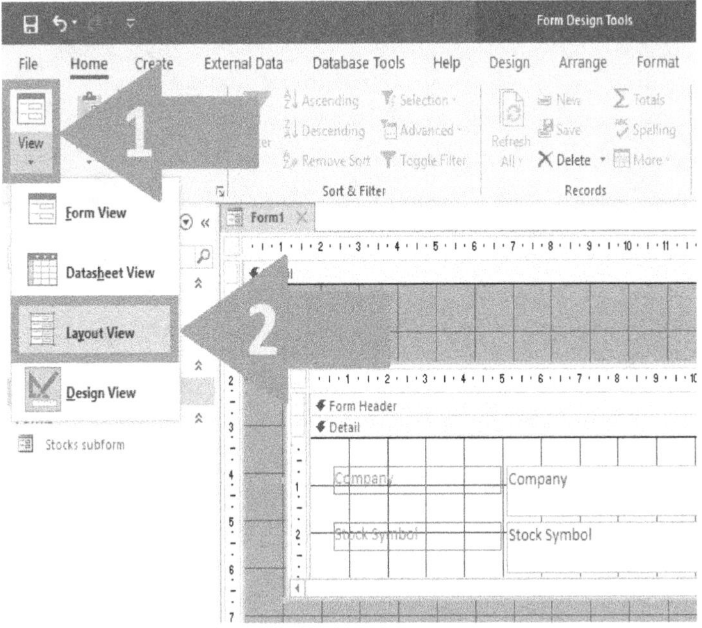

Fig.4h

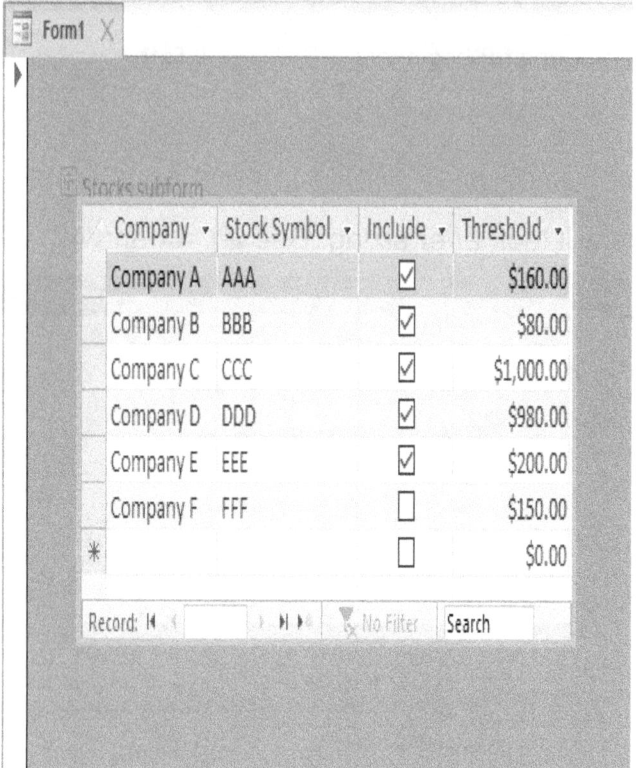

Fig.4i

Now we change our view to forming a view, which will become the user's interface view. See fig. 4j

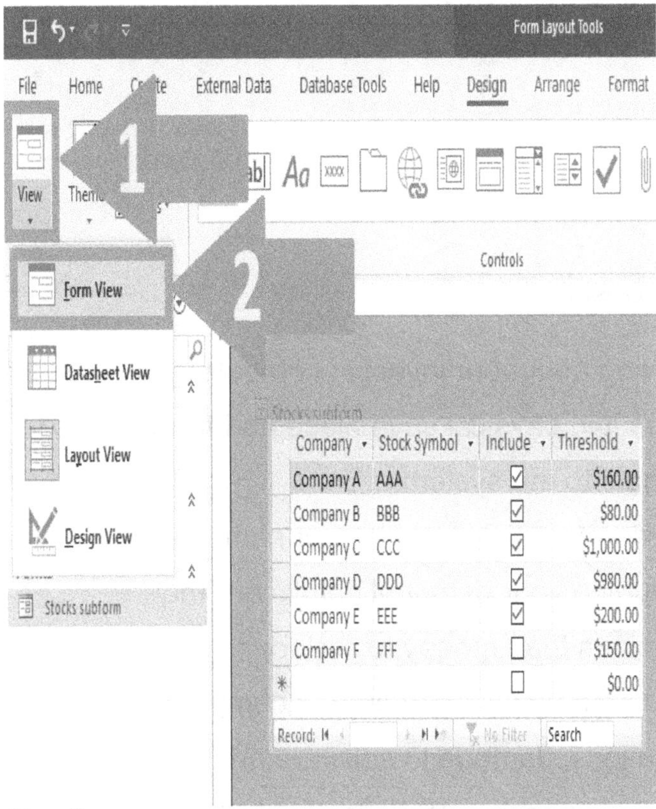

Fig.4j

It's important to note that under the above view, the user can add or delete or even change something from the sub forms they must refresh the pc. Also, the user will be capable of changing the tables' values but won't be able to change the query result. The above steps will be repeated to add the price sub forms.

Chapter 11

Computer security

Synopsis

Having bought or invest in computer you need to
keep it in physical save place and from any
threats to the system.
Remember, the data on your computers
including your personal details are more
precious than money to replace it.
The primary aim is to protect computer against
data loss, damage to software and equipment.
There are many ways that computer can be
attacked and information stollen. Network
resources could be stollen without your
knowledge.
It is therefore to protect the data and the
network. Configuration is one way of securing
your computer.
Set and update programs and operating system.
Updates regularly the antivirus and anti-spyware

Do investigate manufacturers website and try to
the best and affordable security protection

In an organisation you must have security policy
and a clear and concise statement of which all
employee must and I adhere to.

The network in business is more vulnerable to
being attacked.

Within the organisation employee who have
access to the data and equipment may still the
equipment themselves.

Employee may have malicious threats caused
damage. Possible damage to data and
equipment accidentally.

Attacker can use some cold to still information
from the computer without your knowledge.

Outsiders can use sophisticated means.

When you have security policy make sure that
employee understand them. State what is
acceptable for using computers.

The condition of the install the devices.

Protect hardware such as Modern and access
points software. Administrator must keep secrets
some information from employee.

Emergencies procedure

What steps to take in case of emergencies such as who to contact.
Decide on your media, vendors of information to share with your customers.
Increase of fire what location to use and what procedure after emergency.

Chapter 12

Attack on Computer

Virus.

Is malicious software(code) that can copy itself
and infect computer.
There being virus are ineffective and others can
cause serious damage to the data files to be
corrupt and can damage the operation system or
erase files. The problem is that they can be
install up without the knowledge of their own all
user or computer can be affected when opening
the email, storage media, USB or cd/DVD which
carries virus
During the process of files transferring or
responding to instant messaging the email is the
easiest to spread the virus from one computer to
another.

Could corrupt the hard drive. The virus is sometimes used to record keystrokes that is the key board some virus known as Steath virus can infect computer and lay dormant until someone by the creator to carry out instruction of damage or record.

Virus protection.

Anti- virus is a software or program which when install will detect, remove or disable not just virus but also whence and Trojans.

 The anti-virus run automatically monitoring and attack when attacker takes place the order use is one but the software quarantine the virus
it is advisable to run antivirus to clean an unwanted software as proportion.
Installation of antivirus software have specific expiry dates so one can set the computer to automatically install new and latest parties, update organisation must make employee aware of the dangers of opening email attachments

Worms.

This is a small program or software that are mainly inherent in the network .

It can replicate itself or code like binary fission similar to bacteria causing harmful to the network because by attaching itself to the network it can consumes the network bandwidth.

Bandwidth

Bandwidth: is quantity of data being transmitted within a specific time period

Worm is different from virus because it can infect the host without the need to attach to a program. It can be removed with anti-virus.

Trojan

A small software or program code which gives appearance as friendly harmless, but in fact it can cause serious damage such as deleting files or damaged files on a computer. It can reproduce itself and spread to other computers. Trojans can be deleted using antivirus software

Malware.

Our malicious software designed to infiltrate and causing serious damage to a computer possible the operating system. Usually install to the computer system without the knowledge of the user.

There are a few types of malware namely spyware, and well, Grayware, phishing.

Adware.

normally infected the computer when is download software. It is heeding in software that displays advertisements on computer. adware that display in pop up window can open another window. Hence could be difficult to control you can install anti-Adware program or avoid downloading pop-up advertisement.

Spyware.

as per its trade mark, it's spry and monitor the activities of the computer and sends the information to the one who launched it.

Grayware

Grayware is similar to spyware it behave like phishing by tempting you persuade you to provide the attacker with personal information such as personal bank accounts.

Phishing.

Is similar to social engineer, this software persuade the user to provide personal information such as bank account numbers, password or username.

The attacker will trick the user with such as a computer technician or offers, never give sensitive information on the network. You must protect the password to avoid experienced hackers to trace it.

Spam

 simply means an solicitors email popularly known as junk mail. Attacker use span in form of advertisement to attract users the contents may carry or temptation into harmful sites or virus or infected website.

Pop up.

Is also windows with uncontrolled adverts that could fill or cover the screen and fill the email inbox.

Antivirals should be able to stop this.

We have mention data travelling in the network.

We will cover more in details under the heading

network but for now the communication of data transmission are from pot of your computer through the net

SYN Flood.

is another way attacker can send large amounts request network resorting randomly opening the TCP port.

When data is being transmitted attacker can intercept and put false data between the sender and the receiver this is called man in the middle.

Spoofing

is another attackers that may pretend to be trusted computer in order to gain access to the resources on device.

Replay attack.

Is means of attackers used mainly to attract the password attach to the data being sent.

, The attacker can then use it to re-sent to gain access to your computer.

DNS

Another way to map host names to IP address is by attacking the DN S is domain name system, by poison known as DNS poison.

DoS (Denial of Service)

is away attacker can send very large amounts of request to the system resources which eventually deny the user access to normal function of the computer. This is known as denial of service.

DDoS.

Attackers use zombie software, which is infection, this originates from many coordinate sources hence make it difficult to trace the origin of this infected zombies.

Email bomb

Attackers may send a large amount of junk email to the email server preventing the user with normal assets, this is called email bomb

PING OF DEATH pop up

Attacker Might Send repeated large aim to
crush the receiving computer.

This is all ping of death

Chapter 13

Security policy

A security policy must be enforceable on the employee in order to be effective.

Priorities working schedule after emergencies.

To prevent theft, vandalism and data loss you must have security policy to identify hardware and equipment.

Assets, data, infrastructure and computer are interrelated for physical security,

in organisation with a lot of computers, you can restrict unwanted guests on their premises by using security fencing.

You and the organisation must work together for maximum security. If you are a computer technician, your customer will rely on you for advice on security on computer security.

Apart from installation, repair, I just, setting equipment you need to guide against security.

In considering policy for security, the song questions you need to ask yourself. Play a devil advocate. What are the threat. What assets the threats affect. What plans in place in case of security breached.
Process to edit the existing network incidents and network security.
Process of implementing network security.
Allowed and disallowed behaviour of employee on the computer.

Prevention and prohibition

Procedure of what to log and how to store the locks in the security lock files.
In the event viewer, system log files.
Explain account permission, network assets and resources.

Protocols on authentication technologies assess data including smartcards biometrics, password and username.

The security of compliments will be based on the customer needs.

You must periodically research and update current security.

Adding layers of security on a network can make the network more secure.

Take into account the value of the data and equipment with the cost of protection.

You must always discuss security issues with the customer and make note in the journal.

Always remember that your goal is to provide the security system that best matches the customers security policy must be strictly enforceable.

Security of physical equipment hardware.

There are many methods used for protecting physical equipment.

Control access to computer facilities such as biometrics posted security guide, card keys, berg.

Always keep the telecommunication rooms locked.

Protect the network infrastructure including cabling equipment and devices.

Cables locks with equipment
secured cages surrounding desk cases.
Fit equipment with security screws.

Use lockable cases.
Secure storage and transport of backup media.
Protect individual computer.
Use laptop docking stations locks.
Install sensors such as radio frequency identification(REID) tag on equipment.
Provide protection of hardware to prevent on authorised access.

Card keys
 Can store personal data, level of access.
Berg connectors for connecting to a floppy drive.

Biometric sensors.
 This equipment is one of the best security because it identified physical characteristics of the user that is retina of the eye and finger prints.

Bolstered security guard.

Use HD carries.

USB security dangles.

Rights security mix.

Lock.

If a key is lost all identically keyed locks must be

changed.

Conduit

This casing into the war protects the

infrastructure media from damage and on

authorise access.

Video equipment.

 Monitor and record activities. Security fob.....

Which has small radio system that

communicates with the computer over a short

range.

Circuit chips (ICC) connection to a reader direct

or wireless

 smart cards
 Ability to store data.

It always advisable to use two factor
identification for increased security.
To provide security for organisation, you must
disclose the security level require which depend
on the cost of course

Data protection.

Data software protection are worth more than
the cost of the computer hardware.
In addition to what discuss earlier, one need to
protect the data against virus, worms, Trojan,
spyware, grey ware.
All these are created by computer attacker to
destroy data and soft or hardware

.

Chapter 14

Protection

Anti-spyware

this will scan key loggers and other malware including greyware and delete them or disable them.

Password

To get into your computer, you need both password and username so when deciding the password make one that is difficult for anybody's but easy for you to memorise
One way is to have mixture of upper and lower case, use both numbers and alphabets, it is also advisable to change your password frequently such as to 3 months.

Password protection

There are two types or levels to protect the password.
Set the BIOS so that it cannot be changed without the actual password.

Login

This method prevent anyone without the appropriate password to access the network on your computer.

Encourage employees to use password standards which is another protection and avoiding other uses from writing down your password.

You must set the rules of the password example you may choose the computer will be locked out if someone try say three frail attempt.

You can set the computer to remind you the expiry date of the password so that you can change it.

A large organisation you must have a security policy which include password. You can have password use for guest example and accountants. This must be changed frequently. For more secure you must have your password encrypted which means security future that attached a cold to password so that only the authentic user can log into the computer this is more secure because any time have 1st to decode the encryption before attempting to trace the password.

Username

You must choose username which is easy for you to remember but difficult for someone. If you miss taking to someone to guess collect. You must change it immediately.

When you use data encryption you are in effect using quotes and ciphers in most cases it may not be possible to justify the cipher data on time to do anything else.

Event logging.

In order to monitor or ditch any activity on the network, you must enable the invent logging. In a large company the computer administrator often check the invent logging to determine if an attacker have gained access to your network of the computers.

Encode

When data is being transferred in the network one protect it with an encode.

There are various means of encoding using hashing or hash encoding is another way to make sure the data is not intercepted by the computer during transmission Hashing is a method of providing numeric value that is only for the data being transmitted by using mathematical functions. This function is one way and make it impossible or difficult for someone to interfere with the message.

There are two popular encryption use symmetric encryption is a way whereby both ends the sender and receiver use identical keys to quote and decode the data.

Asymmetric encryption

require a private and public keys. The sender uses the private key to send the message which must be kept private to the sender. The public keys can be giving to anyone who wish to decode the sender's code and in fact can be distributed or sent by email.

SHA and MD5

SHA and MD5 are two forms of hashing. Another secure way of sending data is VPN which stand for virtual private network. The data is secured with encryption the transmission data travel in a like pipeline called secure tunnel.

Physical Human.

Social engineering.

Do not give up your username and password. Escort on expected visitors, then will use all excuses to gain access to the most sensitive area, they could be con men.
It is very important not to give your password to anybody in your work as they could use it to cause damage and the administrator will put the blame on you. In a small or large office, developed a habit of locking your computer in a chain and switch it off to protect the computer and your password and username.

Chapter 15

Security on the Web

All computers are most vulnerable if connected to the WWW says the whole world computer attackers can affect users

The VPN.

Is used often by business people and resources mainly in LAN local access network.

TCP/IP or OSI.

TCP stand for transmission control protocol which control all the communication in the nets. The port and during transmission of data are also vulnerable to attacker.

ActiveX.

This small program control in activity on their webpage. This Microsoft to make attack to download small program or apex before gaining access to the full function of the computer.

Java scrip

is term used to describe it program language and allow small program to run within web browsers such as calculators. Java scripts is a programming language and inter-react with hypertext mark-up (HTML) language use to browse Internet. Unfortunately attackers may use active X, Java or Java script to install program on the computer

Back up.

Back up is a means of copying the data on the computer onto a media and store in safe place. Protect data loss.

Reason, data is precious to the computer and if is lost through many ways such as computer physically stalling attackers corrupting or damage the data, fire, flood or computer failure to respond.

Media for back up include CD DVD USB floppy disk external hard drive on the Internet.

In organisation, it always advisable to store the backup in offsite storage location so that in case of fire or theft the computer can lay their hand on the data and restore or reinstall on to other computers.

Backup procedure must be included in the organisation security.

Backup can be performed by using the command line or using NT back in the command. Which needs to be set up in the Windows backup utility. You must be aware that NT backup, cannot be used to store files.
The storage environment for backup media must be in physical security and climate controlled.
In a large organisation, backup could take a long time due to network congestion has you must decide when the network transmission is low especially for emergency backup since the last full backup.

There are different type of backup.

Full back up

or emergency backup by selecting all files since
it was last backup so that you do not have
duplicates. In domestic usage, you might be able
to use the previous media to back up all the files
at least once a month in addition to regular daily
backup the organisation may use.
External hard drive making sure the file names
and dates which will make it easier to retrieve.

A differential backup

this backup consist of files which have been
created and all file audited since the last full
backup It does not Mark files as having been
backup or not reset archive bit.

Incremental backup.
This consists of backing up all the files and
folders that have been created or modified since
the last full backup. The files are thus marked as
backup.

Daily backup.

Backup all files that have been created or modified on the day.

Copy Backup.
It is always advisable to copy the backup and store them in different location or the chairman or director or administrator's house.

Backup password

to protect the backup you must create a password which is not the same house to gain access to the computer which must be entered before the data is stored on the media.

Online backup.

Online backup has it prone and cons; is easy to store but vulnerable for everyone in the world who have computer Knowledge to gain access. It is therefore imperative to have strict policy or the organisation protocol.
Make it difficult with tights password and username.

File system.

There are two main file system in computer depending on their security. Volume of files, efficiency, reliability,

FAT 32 with less security can be convert or upgrade to NTFS. You must be careful before converting because it is not reversible.

FAT32.

This stand for final allocation table; the operating system uses this to store information about location of the store file on a disk.

The file is installed in track "o" on the disc. It can be used with Windows 9598 ME which can be read or written Linux, Mac operating systems uses it as well. It can only hold files of 4GB files or 32GB volumes. It has maximum of 4.17 files per volume. Do not record file transfer history for use in reconstruct ion after errors, large clusters does waste space.

NTFS

New technology file system. This is system that
provide improved forts tolerance over traditional
file systems and offer better security.
Unfortunately this is only compatible with
Windows vista, XP, 200 and N T
But Linux/Unix are read only NTFS it has a
huge file size limit of about 16 terabyte files or
256 telebyte volumes.
It also have 4.29 billion (4, 294, 967, 295.)
The file size are very efficient because it has
smaller clusters which allow it to use more of the
available space. It also have built in compression
maximise space. It is very reliable because it
includes Journaling to rebuild after errors

Signature files.

Virus, worm's, spyware adware, greyware have
different patterns in delivering the code on the
Lan which is local area network and Internet.
The pattern of analysing the are called
intersections are called signatures on files
signatures file are always changing our specific
on the type of malicious code pattern example
virus and are attached to the anti-virus

To have authentic signature files, always retrieve it from the manufacturers websites to make sure the virus had not corrupted.

Downloading signature files from the manufacturer website to multiply down load sites are terms as

Mirrors

Make sure the Mirrors. Site are legitimate and not corrupt.

This is the Procedure to follow.

Set Windows to restore point.

Open the anti-spyware or antivirus program.

Select the update control button.

Use the updated program to scan your computer.

Print or check the report for viruses and other malicious attack which might have escaped treatments and delete them.

Always set the antivirus and anti-spyware to automatically updates or to remind you to download and to install.

Security settings.

As an administrator or use, you may decide the access you wants and individual or group to specific files or folders in the hard drive. You could grant this by configuring what level of permission to allow

Both folders and file permissions include read, write, modify, read and execute, full control

Folders.

Permission to modify gives assets to delete and perform any permitted actions.

Permission to read include access to read all files and subfolders in the folder,

permission to write allow assets to create new files and so folders within the folder, view folder ownership permission charge attributes names of the files and subfolders within the folder.

Read and execute access to folders and subfolders and files. This is full permission because the user have complete authority to the content of the folders and files.

Files permission

Full control gives access to change permission, in effect take ownership plus perform any actions permitted by all other NTFS files

Modify files stop

Gives permission to modify and delete the file, write permission and read and execute permission.

Read only

Is to view the file attributes ownership and permission.
Right;.. Can't change attributes over rights the file, view ownership and those given permission up.

Wireless security.

Wireless is very vulnerable since more people in the world can attempt to attack unprotected computer network.

WEP

Stand for wired equivalent privacy..

This provide encryption the broadcast data between the wireless access point and the user.

The WEP configuration use a 64-bit or 128-bit encryption key.

Wi-Fi (WPA) is protect assets,

It is a security standard for wife wireless technology. This provided better encryption and authentication than WEP and normally supports robust encryption and provide higher level of security.

Wi-Fi is brand name originally licensed by the Wi-Fi alliance to define the embedded technology of a Wi-Fi network which is based on the IEEE802.11 specification.

SHA and MD5

MAC media access control is used for address filtering and restrict computer access to their wireless access point.
In effect it prevents on authorise use from assessing the network. Up however it is always vulnerable and must be used with other security filtering

MAC sub layer handles access to share media which include token passing or contention base. There is rules for alternating the use of the medium on LAN.

SSID

this stand for service set identifier broad casting. The SSID is a unique identifier it usually use for network name which is used by wireless devices to connect to wireless access points.
It is an reliable network security. If one turned off the SSID the network is likely to be disappeared. Wireless antennae this is mainly used to obtain better signal. Install an antenna with a pattern that serves your network..

Accounts.

Computer technology for accounts is mainly defined different level of access to data example the bookkeeper or accountant may only be giving accounts for payroll whilst director and chairman of the company giving accounts for staff meetings, bookkeeping

In a large office group permission two specific files. It is advisable to disable access when an employee leaves a new employee who require the use of previous employee data can be made possible by re-able the files. One can create temporary guest accounts if he or she need access to the network depending on the expansiveness of what the person needs access for.

It is better to suspend the accounts until new guests come in. To get to the specific files you could use protection example double protection.

Fire wall

this is access server all routers to act as a buffer between the private and the public network is very tight. Life most security device it is recommended to use firewall in conjunction with another security. You can use fire wall to protect both data and equipment use on network.

Fire wall modes

there are different ways that firewalls can filter network data traffic depends on how you configure the firewall software..

It opens all close the points for various programs which then creates restrict security policy. And denies outside users from connecting to the network segments or to a computer. This means the packets will denied if not permitted. However a permissive security policy and allow access through all ports except those configured to deny setting on your computer when you purchase new in order to avoid attack gaming are access. Packets is information which has had that control the data during transmission. It is sometimes referred to network layer of the data the logical group information at various layers may have the tense datagram frame, message and segments are used.

Proxy or gateway firewall it protects computers within the network by continuing inspecting all packets and traffic and denies or allow packets based on configured political or rules.

Stateful packets inspection.

This keep track of the packets transmitting within the network connection. Packets which are not part of the known connection are not allowed back through the firewall.
Packets with header as and descend in the TCP/IP and OSI layers.

Hardware firewall.

This is where firewall inspect the data packets from network before they reach the computer or device. Hardware firewall are freestanding unit which means it does not use the resources of the computer that it protect. Normally store on notice it uses dedicated hardware. It can protect multiple computers at the same time.
There is new or little impact on the performance on the computers that it protects. Initial cost can be costly.

Software firewall.

Is a small program on the computer that filters or inspect data packets within the network. When install it can reduce the computer performance because the firewall uses the resources CPU of the computer.

Window XP operating system has software firewall embedded in it.

It is available as third-party software it only protects only the computer it is installed on.

One can configure it in two ways automatically to configure this the user is prompted to 3 questions namely unblock, ask me later, keep blocking. If the firewall has not been configured before this question may be from virus or worm. That has infected the operating system.

Manual setting.

User can add this program or pots that the application in use on the network software firewall. To add software firewall program Start, control panel, security centre, exception, add programme.

To disable the firewall

start, Control Panel, security centre, Windows firewall click on disable.

Chapter 16

Operational system

Operating system computers is equivalent to
organisation when everything that goes on within
the computer or other rely on the policies and
the structure of the operating system.
Why every organisation provide interface
between them and the public hence operating
system is the interface between the user and the
computer. If there is not operating system then
there will be no computer. Operating system
controls all the hard workers software and
applications or programs
What every complexity of the organisation the
operating system controls it so is computer
operating system. Operating system controls the
hardware access, provide a link between the
hardware and the applications, creates a firing
system to store data, manage files and folders,
manage the application for the programme
provide use interface and interpret the uses
command.

Types of operating system.

This include Apple Mac operating system(O),UNIX,LINUX, Microsoft windows include 2000 professional, Windows vista home basic, window Vista business and window Vista Premium.

One of my students sked me " which is more important, operating system or motherboard or CPU". I threw the question to the class and majority got it right that is operating system because without it there will be no computer control.

OS requirement

Minimum requirements for operating system.(OS)

For operation system to work or to accept installation then must be a minimum requirement depending on the type (OS). Example Linux require a minimum of 486 or greater of CPU,

RAM must be 32 MB and hard disk space of 3.5 GB

UNIX

UNIX this require run of 64M be or more and hard disk space of up1G.It is important to know that Linux is a version up new of pop UNIX . The name of who developed it is Linus Torvalds in 1991 but Unix came to the market in 1960.Such as Red hat, Caldera, Suse., Dibeon and Slackware. UNIX This is a proprietary operating system.

Linus

Linus is regarded as open source program meaning it allowed developers to download at considerable low-cost of the source code to be distributed and changed by user as a free download UNIX and Linux do not support CD or DVD Mac OS X.

The required minimum of CPU must be power PC G3, G4,G5 and run of 256 MB, had disk space of 3.0GB

It will operate CD and DVD. There is built in display or Apple supplied video card supports.

The minimal requirement of operating system in Windows there are various types of windows, 2000 is the order which has been replaced by XP, XP 64-bit edition. This is order and only computers with 64-bit processor.

XP tablet PC

XP tablet PC edition support tablet.

Windows XP media Centre used for computers for watch movies, games or music.

XP Home edition.

Used on home computer not suitable for business as it does not have high security allowing spyware, virus, Trojan to invade it.

Window XP professional

Window XP professional is used for business. Because it facilities to connect to the business server on network and is most popular use. The minimum requirement of window XP RAM of 12 8MB or more hard disk space, it support CD, see our wrong and DVD drive, support use of keyboard and mouse.

The CPU must be into Pentium or Celeron family
or AMD, K6/Athlon/Duron family compatible,
single or dual processor,300MHz or higher.

How operative system works

Windows operating system is universally use so
let us look at their futures. In relation to enhance
security ,EFS support's carrier borne CPU
support, network sharing and remote desktop.

Window 2000, XP, professional and
Window XP Home edition,

Window 2000 support all the features except
remote which you need to add on.
Window XP media Centre edition and window
XP professional support all the features.
Window XP Home edition, only support network
sharing. So if you intend to purchase or a gift
from someone, always ask the operating system
installed to include floppy disk 3-point 5 Floppy
drive

Chapter 17

How operating system works.

Hardware.

In order for operating system to manage the application or program and hardware on the communicate with in-store hardware, the manufacture include a small program called device driver in the hardware. When the programme is installed by the operating system it also install the device driver which enable the operating system to communicate with the hard ware.

The device driver must be compatible with the type of operating system install in your computer. (PnP) Plug and Play is an technology that allows a computer to automatically configure the device that connects to it.

The operating system install both the hardware and the device driver in order for the operating system to communicate with install hardware.

Registry

In computer, there is registry which is described as a system wide database used by the Windows operating system to store information and settings for hardware, software, users and preference on a system.

One of the function of operating system is to configure the device driver and update the registry database.

In order for the operating system to manage files and folders it allocates space or structure on the hard disk drive to store the files and folders.

A fire is a computer block of logically related data that is giving a single name and is treated as a single unit.

Programme our directories and the operating system organise it in such a way that there is easy access to retrieve when needed.

Directory .

Is a huge file that organise other small files in hierarchy structure and its provide space to store data in the Windows file management system

DOS

The programme and the data files are grouped together in the DOS file system.

Sub directories.

Sub directories is when a directory is kept inside another directory.

Folder.

This computer name for directory hence subdirectory is called subfolder.

In order for human use to communicate with hardware and software, the user have two choices

CLI and GUI

Almost all operating system have both CLI and GUI facilities.

CLI (Command Line Interface)

Is a command line program that accepts text input to execute operating system functions. this is user interface that requires commands to be entered manually on the command line that is the user typed command.

Historically In the 1960s, using only computer terminals, this was the only way to relate with computers. In the 1970s and 1980s, command line input was commonly used by Unix systems and PC systems like MS-DOS and Apple DOS.

GU I. (graphical user interface)

The second user interface is graphical user interface this allows the user to navigate through the operating system using icons and menus on the monitor screen.
The GUI is a form of user interface that allows users to interact with electronic devices through graphical icons and audio indicator such as primary notation, instead of text-based user interfaces, typed command labels or text navigation. GUIs were introduced in reaction to the perceived steep learning curve of command-line interfaces (CLIs), which require commands to be typed on a computer keyboard

What happened when a program or application is installed.

Application software program that perform a specific function by accepting input from the user and then manipulating it to achieve a result, known as the output. This means when you use the mouse to navigate on the monitor screen your request or command such as print, fax, are produced which is known as output.

Application software program include word processor, database, spreadsheet, games, operating system ensure that the programme has enough resources to operate when you say use the command line.
All the application are loaded into the RAM.

API.

Application program interface is a set of tools, routines and protocols used to develop software applications that will be compatible with an operating system example of API

Open GL.

This built into Windows software to improve performance especially for multimedia graphics. If you like movies and games then this open GL is a must.

DIRECT X.

This are collection of different type of A PL performing multimedia tasks. This is specifically for Microsoft windows.

All computers developers have to abide special guidelines so that the programme is compatible to the operating system, manufacturers use this guidelines to produce their products.

One assess the capability of operating system by the term used in computer language as multi user, Multi-tasking multi-processing and multi-threading

Multi user

If two or more people can you use the same program and peripheral devices which include printers fax email at the same time then the computer is multi-user.

Multi-tasking

Is when the computer is positioned to operate more than one program at the same time. This is when one is working on word then command spread sheet or database on at the same time. Normally one may minimise one or two programme to have the third one on screen to work with.

When more than one or two or more CP you in the computers and the operating system allow all the programs to share the CPU this tasking is call multi-tasking

Multi-threading.

Is a built-in mechanism in the operating system that allow the program to be broken into smaller and to load them when needed.

Mode

CPU operation depend on the Mode, you will find that as operating system advance basically all modem computers have facilities for multi-tasking, multi user, multi-processing, multi-threading. The capability of CPU and the operating system determine the mode. There are four modes namely real mode, protected mode, virtual mode and capability mode.

Real mode

Computers operating in this mode use one program and IMB memory at one time and only use 16-bit operating system the programme has assess the memory hence any Errol in the memory affect the entire computer. And stop the computer responding that is it freezes the computer

A computer that the CPU can have access to all the wrong in the hard disk is all protected mode this operate on 32-bit memory, drivers and permit transference of inputs to output it also allow multiple programs simultaneously. It is important to bear in mind that all computers have specific assigning resources and the protective mode protect this a sign resources from being used by other program. Example are window XP and window 2000 have protected mode.

Virtual real mode

When a rear mould application running within a protected mode is the computer operating in virtual rear mode

There are some older version operating system which operates with modern operating system, this oak her when compatibility mode is capable to create an environment version with the operating system to run as if it has same compatibility.

NOS and SOHO

Every human, machines mechanic equipment and computers have capabilities, pebbles and limitation. The two main computers use our desk top and network.

Desk top.

This is used to portray file system.
Every human, machines mechanic equipment and computers have capabilities, pebbles and limitation. The two main computers use our desk top and network.

.An desk top consist of pictures called icons
which shows file, folders, and any resources
available to a user in the graphic user interface
operating system.

Desk top computer is designed to fit on top of a
desk, usually with the monitor on top of the
computer as space savings, why as laptop and
mobile, desktop computers and not mobile.
It is suitable for small office or home office
(SOHO) it is mainly for a single user runs single
use program. It has limited security but they are
capable to share files and folders programs.
UNIX and Linux Apple Mac and Microsoft
windows operating system support SOHO

Chapter 18

NOS (Network operating system)

Network operating system is for multiple use with little or no limitation, designed specifically to provide additional network futures. It is use in large office or cooperate. It provide increased security, multiple users, multi user application, robust or redundant. It provide increased functionality up and manageability for networking. It is basically designed specifically to provide networking resources to the user, also capable for server application such as share data bases.

Some network operating systems are.
Windows 2000 server and window server 2003 and window 2010. This Microsoft Windows server use a centralised database storage it is directory of folders that provide storage space of resources and user accounts database called active directory which manage or network resources.

Novel net ware

this network was developed in the 1980s and hence the first operating system to meet operating system requirements.

OS (Operating system)

Operating system must be compatible with any programme that is current or future use and must also support or current and future hardware. This include network facilities, consider the type of network and choose which operating system are available.

To choose operating system, ask yourself a few questions to guide you.
Do you wish to buy off the shelf application or program.
If you decide to purchase of the shelf, you must read the label carefully because it's specify a list of operating system capability.
Is it for multiple or single user do you need network now all future, if you decide is for networking future then you must wait to bracket if finance is a problem now until you can afford operating system with network facility.

Do you propose to share files and folders directories with other computers on the network? You must make sure that the practicability of fire formats is the same operating system that the order data file sharing computers if budget constrained investigate what you want to use the computer for and consider the type of programs or application.

If however you wish to customised the application, then the program will specify what type of operating system is compatible with it. It is very important to take into account minimum hardware and come back ability which must be met before you can install the operating system

RAM, hard disk drive, CPU video adapter.

Sometimes it is cheaper to upgrade RAM, hard disk drive, CPU video adapter.

Check the package and you will see a list of minimum requirements. This is called hardware compatibility list (HCL) you can always check update list on the manufacturers websites. There is possibility that existing hardware is not on the list then you will need to upgrade the component to meet the need.

Network access and security.

To have redundant storage system such as backup or RAID
RAID. (redundant Array off independent disc)
It provide thought tourism's to prevent data loss in the event of a disk drive failure on a network server. RAID is sometimes known as redundant array of in expensive disc.
Network operating system provide several rules governing network which are acceptable within the network. In computer language is protocols which must be abide by the network to function

PROTOCOL

Former description of a set of rules and conventions that govern how devices on a network exchange information. Or is field within an IP data ground that indicates the upper layer which is the fourth protocol that sent the datagram

IP (Internet protocol)

Is usually referred to an address that is unique number that devices use in order to identify and to communicate with each other on a computer network utilising the Internet protocol IP standard.

There are codes on the network which are controlled by the protocols a use by the next working operating system which intent provide the user with all the Internet services example, email, file transfer, word browsing and complement being giving automatic IP address. All this protocols may be to advance but lend them or must know what they are for. Some of the network protocols or rules will have to work to obtain the function working. They are normally abbreviating but learn what they mean.

DHCP. (Dynamic cost control protocol)

Dynamic cost control protocol is a software utility that automatically assign IP addresses to the user devices usually in the large network.

HTTP. (Hypertext transport protocol)

Hypertext transport protocol is the standard used to transfer information on the WWW world wide web. Is communication protocol that establishes a request connection on the Internet or how files are exchanged on the web.

FTP (File transfer protocol).

File transfer protocol. It consist of rules governing how files are transferred and manipulate. It allows simultaneous connection to remote file system.

POP. (post office protocol)

post office protocol. Is protocol used to retrieve email from your mail server. It has various version in the version being used in 2013 is 3.

You will need to be careful because up also stand for point of presence which relates to point of interconnection between communication facilities provided by the telephone company and the main distribution facility of the building

DNS (Domain name services)

Domain name services is a protocol that resolve URL for website with their IP addresses or provide a way to map friendly host names. Here again you may have DNS up poisoning which is hackers use to change the DNS records on a system. Want to false servers where the data is recorded.

DOMAIN

it is logical group of computers and electronic devices with a common set of rules and procedures administered as a unit

Chapter 19

Installation of operating system.

Operating system set up; is the term used to describe installation and first boot of the operating system. As the operating system is being installed on the hard drive, let this stand how to prepare the hard drive. There are a few technical technology we can't avoid.

Hard disk.

before install operation one need to divide or partition the hard drive disk in order to choose which space you wish to install.

Partition.

The process is called format and after formatting it is ready for the part of partition to hold the files system established operating system. The process of partition and for formatting is called hard disk setup

Each section of the partition have specific name and specific data that can be stored.
this is the term used to divide the hard disk memory into isolated or logical sections, once the hard disk is partition, each partition will behave like a separate disk drive. There will be specific name for the partition. Once you have divide or partition you must prepare it in computer protocol before you can store any data on.

Active partition.

Partition on a hard disk drive that is set as bootable partition to start computer. It is mainly used to store operating system for the computer it is important to know that only one active partition or bootable portion on one hard disk. This means if you wish to have more than one operating system you will need to install another hard disk in the computer.

Primary partition.

This is the first partition on the hard drive it is important that this partition cannot be subdivided into smaller sections that you can have up to 4 primary partition on 1 Hard drive

Extended Partition

This is normally the second partition on the hard drive and it uses the remaining space after primary and active partition.
The good thing is unlike the primary, you can divide extended partition into smaller, this smaller partition or sections are called logical drive. On the hard drive you have cylinder and cluster.

Cylinder.

All line railway tracks on the hard disk on top of each other to form cylinder shape. Collectively, the same track and all platters of multi-platter hard drive.

File allocation or cluster

Smallest unit of space used to store data on a disc

Sector. A segment within a track on the disc and is the smallest unit that can be accessed on a disk.

Drive Mapping

Is the process of assigning a letter to a logical or physical drive.

Do not worry about all this technology unless you want to be computer technician.

Most operating system I is it to install, just put the CD and it will ask you a few questions during the process just for you to answer them and installation more complete automatically up.

Let's look at the process of installation of operating system using window XP.

Window XP Professional.

Chapter 20

 Four different ways to Install an Operating System on a Computer

There are 4 ways to install an operating system

Method 1 of 4: Installing Windows 10. Create a Windows Installation Media. If you order Windows 10 for a new PC build,

Method 2 of 4: Setting Up Windows 10. Verify your region and keyboard input. When Windows restarts, it will ask you few questions to answer

Method 3 of 4: Installing MacOS. Back up your files. It's recommended that you back up all files and data you want to

Method 4 of 4: Setting Up MacOS. Select your country and click Continue. Use the menu to select

The 4th installation method needs minimum indirect action. Once you answer the question it will complete automatically. This is also a term as typical installation hence you are more likely to succeed compared to custom installation. The questions include you are prompted to provide information such as Stannard and formats that defined type of currency either pounds or dollars and which country, and numerals, language that you want input, name of the user and company name. Product key these come with the purchase. What name you wish to call the computer, administrator password, date and time settings

Customer installation.

Customer installation is normally used in corporate and large organisation to meet larger network.

During the customer set up, you have only two screens. The first one is to put regional setting to customise it; the second screen is network settings to customise. The wizard will prompt you for more details information so that the operating system can customise as per your requirements either for large network administrator or individual.

Although way to install customise is by using answer file with predefined settings and answer two questions during the wizard process.

By so doing fop you can install operative system on more computers at the same time without you being there.

At the same time you can setup automatic update.

Now let go back of how systematic installation. Up for large network this is the quickest as you can install the window XP professional too many computers.

 The method include.

on attended installation

network by using answer file or

image-based installation

by using Sysprep and disc image which copy the image of the operating system onto the computer at the same time.

Sysprep is a system preparation used to install and configure it operative system on multiple computers.

RS remote installation services.

This is done by downloading from the network.

Operating features using system Management server which is more quicker.

systematic installation

The first stage is to put the CD or DVD in the floppy disk.

This will then partition the hard drive and format it as discussed earlier.

To prepare system for operating system formatting configurated and data file.

Configuration is service management or element management service usually use with
 G UI graphic user interface.

G UI graphic user interface

GUI (graphic user interface.)

This interface allow the user to navigate through the operating system using icons and menus it provide graphical representation or icon of all the files folder and programs on computer.

There are two main files FAT 32 and NTFS .
File is a directory or a block of logical related data that is given a single name and is treated as a single unit.
FAP 32 stand for file allocation table that the operating system uses to store information about the location of the files stalled on a disc in track zero of the hard disk.
A partition which has at partition size up to 2TB or 2048GB gigabyte .

NTFS new technology file system.

This have file level security with much approve fought tolerance compare the F AT32. It can support up to 16 exabyte of partition size. It also have extended attributes one of the question after partition is the wizard will ask if you wish default setting or customise setting.

Unattended Installation.

This is the easiest custom installation of an operating system without much installer intervention and is done on the network the method is to create answer file called on attend txt. Within the deploy cab. Normally on window XP professional CD. The answer file use a program called set upmgr.exe.

An answer file contains three determine settings and questions and answers which are require by the operating system setup wizard.

The procedure is to put the CD in the optic drive, few questions come up, after answering them run the on attended. bat on the computer which will then prepare partition and formatting and install the operating system automatically from the network server.

 The other way is to create a boot disk use it to boot up the computer and it connects to the distribution share

Which is computer that distribute the operating server onto the computer on the server. Next line the last thing to do is to run the batch file which then import the operating system from the network to install on the operating system on the computer or computers

Images -base installation (Cloning)

This is also call disc CLONING used by police and FBI. It is by creating the image of the hard disk onto a disc. To do this
completely confident one computer which has the operating system setup and fully operational this is called the master installation.

Run SYSPREP which is system preparation.

Using 1/3 party disc cloning program prepare the complete image of the master computer.
Then the image onto DVD or CD.
Copy the image onto the distributing server.
This image can then be copied from the server onto all computers which have HALs compatibility to complete the installation on as many or multiple computers.

HAL

HAL stand for hardware compatibility layer

which is like a library of hardware drivers that communicate between the operating system and the install hardware

Security Identifier(SID)

is created by this setup which install hardware drivers, user accounts is created and configured network, setting.
Once the image has been copied, brought up the computer for the first time. If some of the setting such as domain membership, computer name, have not been configured then you will have two do this.

RIS

RIS stand for remote installation service. In tis Is ability to download a Windows operating system through the network and install onto a computer. The organisation administrator can force users to install them.
The only difference from the cloning or image is that with RIS up you do not need disc images

CD or DVD the RIS network have folders that are shared hence our RIS can be used to copy all the Windows operating system files.
Operation system can be loaded on remote boots enable any computer.

(PXE)

By using pre-boot execution environment(PXE) computer that is connected to the network can install operation system by remote book disc or the computer will be able to download with network adaptor.
It is advisable not to use RIS not in large network(WAN) Wide area network as it is design for small network.

SMS (system Management server)

system Management server is a tool in the window XP which allows the computer administrator to manage computers on network. Such as perform inventory management, provide remote control and updates.
SMS Is very powerful and useful to on the windows to thousand and three, it allows many

computers to have operating system installation of all the user network which include LAN local area network or WAN wide area network

LAN (LAN local area network)

LAN is a communication network that covers a small geographical area and is under the control of a single administrator.

WAN (WAN wide area network)

WAN is data communication network that says a wide area and uses transmission devices which are provided by common carriers such as frame relay, SMDS,X.25 are all example of WAN
When you put the windows XP professional it will give you three choices.
setup XP to do this choose or click setup or install the XP operating system by pressing enter.
Repair XP chosen this world by pressing R .and install repair menu will be used to open recovery console

Quit=PressF3 will quit or not install the window XP.

During the installation you will need to create accounts or administrator accounts. The operation system comes with predefined accounts or default called administrator, after installation you must change the name to administrator account that nobody know except you. Failure to change will invite hackers to break or invade your computer and steal all your data. The administrator account is for extra security and key for your computer.

During installation just before is finished you will be prompted for the new site account which can be created at any time even after you have finished installation. User account has fewer permissions than administrator account. You can create more than one user accounts example for ignition or visitors working on your computer. Do not let him or her know your user account or changed it when he finished do not give anybody the administrator's account

Chapter 21

Installation of second operating system in the computer

To have more than one operating system on a single computer you need more than one hard disk Or hard drive capable to have more than one active partition

You need to investigate because some software may require newer version whilst others require older version

When the computer is booted the boat.ini file will be aware that the computer has more than one operating system, one of them will be set as default, and a default time is also set up usually 30 seconds or you can change this as is the time you allow yourself to choose which operating system you wish to use. When the time is lapse and you have not chosen, the default operating system will be used to boot up the computer

You can always go into the boots.ini file and change the time longer or shorter 10 to 15 seconds.

The second operating system can be installed in the second active . Partition hard drive. Which the book boots files are automatically installed on the active partition of the hard drive.

To edit the boot-in file.

Right click my computer, then properties, then advanced tab, then stepped up and recovery setting and click edit

Chapter 22

Upgrading Operating System

There are many reasons are you so wish to upgrade operating system possible due to demand on a new come up the market or for faster operating system. Whatever reasons follow the following guidelines.

The operating system in the computer to perform automatic download to update or download but not to install. Which gives the user opportunity to investigate the usefulness before installation.

Before upgrading, system, check the minimum specification required.

Check the hardware compatible list (HCL) to ensure that the hardware is compatible with the new operating system.

Backup all data before upgrading the operating system just in case there is problem with the installation.

Microsoft windows have a utility known as upgrade adviser which can be used to scan the system for compatibility issues to help yourself decide upgrade as you will have reports for any problem or not

Most upgrade fail due to incapability in the hardware. It's important to know that window 3.1, 95 cannot be upgraded the window XP.

With window work station 4.0 you need service Pack 6 and window 2000 professional can only be upgraded to window XP professional. Window 98, 98SE,Me or can be upgraded this include window XP home or window XP professional.

The process of upgrading a computer system from window 2000 to window XP is quicker than performing a new installation of window XP. The window setup utility replaces the existing window 2000 to window X files during the upgrade process however the application and setting will not change.
There is no charge to download the upgrade advisor from Microsoft website.
Insert the window XP CD into the CD-ROM drive to start the upgrade process. Then select start and then run.
In the run box where D is the drive letter for the CD Rom, type D;/i386/EIN+32 and press enter.
The welcome to the windows XP setup wizard displays.

Choose upgrade to window XP and click next.

The lances agreement page is displayed.

Read the license agreement and if you agree

with the bottom to accept it.

Click next the upgrading to the windows XP

NTFS file system page displays.

Follow the prompts and complete the upgrade

when the install is complete the computer will

restart.

When you insert the CD the Windows setup

wizard may automatically start.

Register boot sequence for window XP.

When successful installation of operating

system, the computer reboots, the first thing you

will be axed by the computer is to register

window XP and also complete the verification,

thus become legal user of copy of the operating

system. It will allow you to download and

upgrade, patches service Pack. You must have

Internet connection to perform this.

Boot evidence

Turn on computer first time after operation

system and is known as cold boot.

A screen which will show you the sequence.

The first thing the computer does is to test it self-known as post or power on first test for all the compliments and each adapter card the computer has BOIS. It may give beats code for any error in any company's or adapter card

BIOS take over after POST which they rate all the setting and save and installed in the complementary metal oxide semiconductor (CMOS) which is low power memory firmware that stalls basic configuration information.

BIOS then boot the computer and locate the master boot record (MBR).

The MBR then locate the operating system boot loader which is called NT loader (NTLDR).

NTLDR control many installation steps example is the NTLDR using boots.ini which gave the user the default time to choose if more than one type of operate chief system.

NTLDR uses NTDETET.com to detect any install hardware.

NTLDR loads theNTOSKRNL.EXE file andHAL.DLL. This are two files that make the call of XP.

NTLDR rate this registrar files and loads devise drivers, choose a hardware profile

NTOSKRNL .EXE start theWINLOGON.EXE program and display the windows login screen.

REGISTRYA very important wish for Microsoft Windows XP boots process and all the files start with HKEY follow by the pats of the operating system under their control. Example

HKEY-current configuration control information relating to all active devices on the system.

HKEY-LOCAL MACHINE information relating to the hardware and software.

HKEY-USERS information about all uses who have locked onto a system.

HKEY CLASSES ROOT information about which file extensions map to a particular application.

As you can see the registrar control every setting in Windows where all information about the computer and operating system are control. Any changes in the computer example programs file, control panel, settings are all stalled in the registrar.

All users of the computer, the registrar recognise this and unique name.

THE NT KERNEL

This is regarded as the heart of all windows operating system.

The name of the files in NT Kernel is called NTOSKRNL.EXE the login file is called WINLOGON.EXE which in turn display on the monitor welcome to window XP.

If a SCSI drive use the boot the computer, Windows or copy the NTBOOTDD.SYS during installation.

The important thing is that if SCSI drives not being used the NTBOoTDD.sys will not be copied.

Chapter 23

Post operating system installation.

After installation the user can modify some settings or information.

MSCONFIG:

This is window utility designed to aid the trouble shooting of the operating system, permits user to set the application that needed to and will run at start up. User can also edit start up.

Start-up applications and simplified control over window services. Provide access to the BOOT.INI.

SYSTEM. INI and WIN.INI.files.

REFEDIT

Is application that allows user to edit the registry.

REGISTRY-this system wide database used by the Windows operating system to store information and settings for hardware, software, users and preferential on a system.

REGEDT32

Was used in window NT. Users can use this as shortcut to Regedit.

Rededit32.exe or Regedit.EXE must be used with care because incorrect use could cause configuration problem which can only be solved by reinstalling the operating system.

Both reg edits 32.EXE and Regedit.EXE run the same program.

Modes

Modes allow us the user to select how you wish to boot the computer windows.

When the computer is started press F8 during the process of booting. It will then open windows advance stacked up. Option menu: safe mode or last known good configuration.

Safe mode

this option allows user to start the computer but the system only loads the basic devices that windows needs to run such a basic components

Keyboard and monitor screen. It is also used for trouble shooting.

Safe mode with network

In addition to loading the basic. Compliments as safe mode, it also loads the drivers for network computers.

Safe mode with command prompt.

This will load the save mode complement and command prompt but not the graphic user interface (GUI)

Last known good configuration

This has the ability to assess a copy of the registrar that was created the last time window was booted and or allow the user to load the setting which were configurated.. Although this is used for troubleshooting, it is more effective if it is applied immediately after computer fails. The registrar may have the configuration with faulty information.

File extension

To identify file type, three or four letters can be added to the file name. Note that filename are not case sensitive that is you can use upper or lower case.

There is maximum of 255 characters to choose from.

The common extension are

.doc = Microsoft word

.txt=ASCII text only

JPG= graphic format

.ppt= Microsoft

PowerPoint.zip= compression format.

Windows does not openly display the file extension but this is likely to cause security problem. It is always advisable to display file extension. The virus writers are able to distribute executable files disguised as a non-executable file.

To show the file extension

Stats menu, control panel, folder option, view and uncheck the hide extensions for files types. Check box.

The bootable is labelled as drive C;/. Directory which uses install data, files, application and configuration.

Most file in the directory structure have file extension as shown earlier.

Attributes

This is just to how the file may be viewed or change. Easy to remember by using RASH

R= the file is read only.

A= the file will be archived the next time disc is back

S+ the file is marked as a system file and warning if an attempt is made to delete or modify the file.

H the file is hidden in the directory display.

VIEW

To view the file names, extensions, attributes use

ATTRIB command   start, run, cmd.

If you get folder, to find the file you are interested in type ATTRIB and filename using wired card888 will review many files in the directory or folder.

To see properties of file rights click then starts then exploring the tools then folder options then view.

Modification of file

You must always back up files before you attempt to modify it in case something goes wrong during the process.

(CLI)Command line interface is for woolly text.

Desk tops.

A desktop is what you see on the screen after meeting. It consist of pictures and icons which assure files folders and in the resources available to a user in a GUI operating system. These can be customised with images sounds and colours in order to personalise the user need. There are five main properties of desktop namely Themes, desk tops screen Saver, appearance and settings.

Customise.

To customise item on the screen such as recycle bin, task bar example point on it right click the item and choose properties.

How to view application on computer.

Click on the start button there are two sties of start menu XP and classic the screen will display all of the application install, list of other element tools for such futures, help centre and system settings, list of recently opened documents.

How to view drives install.

Double click my computer icon. If you wish to customise any of these, computer name, hardware settings virtual memory, automatic update, remote access, launching applications. Point the mouse icon on item and right click and choose properties and then item.

How to launched application.

There are many ways to lunch program.
From click on run, from CM – command line
double click the shortcut icon on the desks top
double click the application executable file
my computer, click the application on the start
menu my network places.

How to view and configurate network connection

point the mouse and right click my network.
Chris is icon on the desktop. This will connect or
disconnect you from the network drive.

Two config rich existing net white connection
Lan wired or wireless LAN connection, right click
my network places and click properties.

Control Panel

the control panel have can be view by double
click the control panel icon. This will show all
futures or controls. The four main categories are

appearance and themes that shows applets look of window

display

task bar and start menu

folder option

adding or removing program, changing settings or security.

All this are called APPLETS which are small program found in the control panel.

Device manager.

Is an application that displays a list of all the hardware that is installed on the system, can also view the values assigned for the IRQ interrupt request, a request from a device for communication with the CPU.

I/O= input /output

DMA direct memory access which is method used by bypassing the CPU when transferring data from the main memory directly to the device.

To activate device manager overview,

start the control panel the system then hardware then device manager then view then resources.

Task manager.

It displays all active currently running applications and identifies those applications that are not responding in order to shut them down. It also provide tools to review the performance of the CPU and the virtual memory, provide information about the network connection.

To view task manager.

CTRL--ALT__DEL--TASK Manager.

Event viewer

This is application that monitors system events, application events and security invent. In short it provide history events.
Invent is network message indicating operational irregularities in physical elements of the network or in response to the parents of a significant task, typically the completion of a request for information,

To view event viewer.

Start the control panel then administrative tools then event viewer.

Remote desktop

This is troubleshooting feature and can be used by windows XP professional. Usually used by technician whereby one computer takes over control of another computer by remote control.

To access

starts then or programme then accessories then communication then remote desktop connection.

Setting

There are a lot of setting for the operating system. This increase the performance of the operating system. This can be changed through this path.

Start then Control Panel the system advanced performance area then settings button.

Add and remove applet

It is recommended to use add or remove programs utility so that the utility can install or remove an application. This is very important as the utility contracts the path used to installed which will make it easier to uninstall. The path start then Control Panel then add or remove programs.

To uninstall an application

To avoid leaving files on the hard drive and unnecessary setting in registry, it is very essential to uninstall property path. To do this

starts then Control Panel them out or removed program.

Disk management

System utility used to manage hard drive and partition such as initialising disks, creating partitions and for mounting partition. This serves is used in windows XP professional.

There are different ways of accessing disk management start then write click my computer then manage them disk management.
Start then settings then Control Panel then administrative tools then computer management. Double click storage then disk management.

System tools

you can assess various tools within Windows need to increase the performance of operating system within Windows example disk defragmenter, virtual memory, disk error checking.

Virtual memory

The tools is a swap file sometimes call page file. Is memory created and controlled by the operating system. It function by allowing the CPU to address more memory that what is install in the computer. Other function is to manipulate free hard disk space to intake more RAM than is actually install in the operating system.

Do not change the setting except the location of the swap file and is administrator job. There are two main ways to access virtual memory

Start then setting them control panel then system then advance tabs then performance options

Start then Control Panel then performance and maintains then system then advanced then performance then setting then advanced.

It is very important to let the windows within the operating system to manage the v virtual memory.

Disk defragmenter

This is a tool within the window operating system that re-arranges the data and rewrite all the files on the hard disk drive to the beginning of the drive, making it easier and faster for the hard drive to retrieve data. The storage of files on the hard drive could be scattered all over the disk, which slow the computer down, because it takes a long time for this section of files.

Disk different mentor re-arranged this file to be contiguous. This allows the computer to find the file quickly and create more space for more file. To access disk defragmenter double click my computer then right click drive then choose properties then tools then click defragment.

Temporary files

10 Ferrari files or those not needed anymore must be deleted to provide space for permanent files and to increase the speed of the computer. To maintain this, it is advisable to delete them at least once a month if you use the computer a lot or every three months to access these files type

C;/temp C;/windows/temp,   C;/document and setting 5user profile 5local settings/temp.

Maintenance service

Computer needs regular service this can be started or initiated if is needed to be for security risk. The up four main service are automatic, manual, disabled, stopped.

Starting not need service will only slow computer service not needed regularly manual

Services not needed regularly must be config relate manually example UPS, print spooler..

You can disable what is not needed.

DGCP(dynamic host configuration protocol).

This software utility is very important because it automatically assigns IP addresses to clients devise in a large network if it is set automatic.

IP stand for Internet protocol address.

This is a unique number that device use in order to identify and communicate with each other on a computer network utilising the internet protocol standard .

Internet Explorer.

The Microsoft browser is embedded in the Internet explorer and contain browser appearance setting. It allows viewing or save.

Internet explorer then tools then Internet option then setting.

Cookie

Text file within the hard disk that allows a website to track the users to that site. The transmission information is between the user browser and web server.

Caching

This is data storage area or to within the internet's Explorer, it helps to provide high speed access for the operating system use to quickly assessing the previously visited websites. This information is stored in the local hard disk cache so if the user wish to visit that site again the Internet explorer will not need to go section for it again. Cache up files could increase due to out dated files; hence it is advisable to refresh all deleted unnecessary files.

To access cache.

From Internet explorer browser then tools then
Internet option. The following are some Internet
explorers configuration options available tabs..
Advanced= used to enable and disable
operational settings of the user browser.
Programme= to set up which programme
windows automatically uses for each Internet
service.
Connection= to set up the Internet connection
settings for the user browser.

Content= to block unwanted websites content
and set identification and personal information.

Privacy= four privacy settings, to block third
party pop ups or cookies.
General= two set home page, view and delete
temporary Internet files and change the browser
appearance setting.

E-mail

Microsoft's Windows operating system use
Outlook express as an email tool.

You need to have your email account with provider. The information needed to install email include, username, outgoing mail server name, incoming mail server name, must decide the type of mail server example pops3 or in, email address and display name.

POP

Post office protocol account password

This is an email protocol used to retrieve email from a mail server there are different version 1to3 or TCP – IP. Once it Is Rickles, the server loses it content. Recent improvement has been able to saved mail on the server for specific time.

IMAP

Internet message access protocol.

This is also used by email clients to retrieve email from server and leaves on the server. IMAP operates the same rate of folders between the server and user.

SMTP

Simple mail transfer protocol.

Email protocol used by severs to send ASCI text messages. It can curry email with pictures and documents when augmented by MIME protocol. SMTP is sometimes used by email users to retrieve messages from an email server. Due to the limited ability to queue messages at the receiving end of protocols such as POP,IMAP are preferring to receive email.

MIME

Multi-Pebbles Internet mail extensions.

This has capability to extend the year mail formats to include text in ASCII standard, as were as other formats such as pictures and world.

PROCESSOR normally used in conjunction with SMTP.

There are other features available to enhance email operation which include email according example HTML plain text on rich text.

I will briefly explain the abbreviation HTML which stand for hypertext mark-up language.

It is page description language used by browsers applications example Mozilla Fire Fox windows Internet explorer.

For Internet explorer, IMAP,SMTP,MIME,POP. They need vertical to travel in which will be discussed under Chapter on networking. But one is TCP. This is Internet protocol for the delivery of data. TCP have facilities for and to and connection, Errol detection, recovery, metering the rate of data flow into the network.

Many standard application such as email, web browsers, file transfer, telnet depend on the services of TCP.

IP= Internet protocol.

The two there are main vertical in the Internet email.

Screen resolution.

The video cuts and monitors affect the contents of the screen and must be set to native resolution or native mode.

Resolution.

Is the number of distinct pixel in each dimension that can be displayed on a computer screen. Higher resolution gives better quality. It sometimes called display resolution.

Refresh rate.

Fullscreen to be steady and clear images one need higher rate of how the image is redrawn. This rate is express in Hertz (H2).

Display colours.

The three basic colours are red, green, and blue which are created according to the intensity and number of colleagues visible on the screen at once this is express by bits. More bit gives yellow quality screen
8-bit colours consist of 256 colours.
65536 colours give high colours all 24 bits.
16 million colours give true colour or 24 bits
16 million colours gives true colour allowing 32 bits processor.

Update

The operating system can be set to update according to your choice.

Automatic whereby you must be specific of date and time.

Download updates for use but not load. In this setting user decide when to load it.

Notify me but don't download or install.

Turn off automatic update

Restore point

Restore points is like storage for the operating system. It is numerically found in Microsoft's Windows ME, XP and Vista operating system. It permits rolling back of the operating system files, registry, keys and programme for installation of previous state in the event of a system failure. Users data is not affected by performing a restore points. It is restore point does not recover personal files that have been corrupted or deleted. It will not save anything in the recycling in.

Prevention and maintainers.

BSoD is known as blue screen of death and cause by malfunction of device driver as result of hardware or software error that could cause the operating system to lock up.
To investigate this one can use the event log or other diagnostic utility within the Windows. The solution could be to update the windows. Install newer patches, investigate the drivers for hardware and software.

Chapter   24

Communication skills.

 What is the best way to communicate with customers?

Speaking directly with the customer is usually the first step.

Whether you are talking with a customer on the phone or in person, it is important to communicate well and to represent yourself professionally.

Successful technicians control their own reactions and emotions from one customer to the next.

Remember this free's at the beginning of your Conversation.

Know all your customer by name

Relate use brief communication to create a one to one collection between you and your customer.

Understand determine the customer's level of knowledge about the computer to know how to effectively communicate with the customer.

After you have listing to the customer explain the whole problem. Beginning with the word lets me see if I understand what you have told me.

This is very effective way that shows the customer that you were listening and are concerned with the issues.

Follow up questions should be targeted roast and question is based on the information you have already gathered specific information.

The customer should be able to answer with all simple yes or no.

You should not interrupt the customer to ask a question or make a statement. This is this mood and this rude and disrespectful.

Be positive when communicating with the customer. Tell the customer what you can do. Do not focus on what you cannot do.

Outline the process to follow before you put a customer on hold. First let the customer finished speaking

Then explain about put on hold and axe permission to do so. If he agrees thank the customer. Some process for transferring the customer call.

Part of technicians job is to focus customer during the phone call When you focus the customer on the problem it allows you to control the hall.

An SLA is typically illegal agreements that contains the responsibilities and liabilities of all parts involved. Some of the content of an SLA usually include the following!

Response time guarantees this often based on of call and level of service agreement.

Equipment and software that is supported. What service is provided. Diagnostics. At every level equivalent parts cost and penalties.

Type of customer

A talkative customer discusses everything except the problem. Uses the call as an opportunity to socialise. It can be difficult to get him for course on the problem.

A rude customer

a rude customer complaints during the call, often make negative comments about products or the service and the technician. Sometimes abusive and uncooperative and get augmented very easily.

Knowledge of the customer.

A customer who have knowledge of the computer want to speak with a technician that is equally experienced in computer, initially they try to control the call and does not want to speak with level I technician.

In experienced customer

inexperience customer has difficulty describing the problem. This customers are usually not able to follow directions correctly and not able to communicate with arrows that they encounter

Do not Axe questions that the customer has already as why describing the problem up.

When dealing with customer, it is important to adhere to that customers SLA'

SLA is contract that defines expectation between an organisation and the service vendor to provide an agreed upon level of support.

There might be exceptional to the SLA. Make sure to follow your company's business rules explained to management should be reserved for special situations for example a long-standing customer or a customer from a very large company might have a problem that falls outside the parameters stated in their SLA. Transfer them to your manager or your management might choose to support the customer for customer relationship reason.

When to follow SLA and to escalate management call centre employee rules

Arrive at your work station on time and Ellie in North to become prepared. Usually about 15 to 20 minutes before the first call.

Often a problem are the expects of a level II technician. In this case the level I technician must be able to transfer the customer's problem descriptions into a succinct sentence of two is entered into work order

when transferring the customer to a level II technician up. So this translation is important so that the technicians can quickly understand the situation without having to axe

the customer the same questions again

Chapter 25

Questions

1. Q what is a common cause of error message "invalid system disc"
2. Q Name one type of PC card
3. Q; How many configuration?
4. Q: which power mode would
5. Q which protocol maps known IP
6. Q which of the following uses the network
7. Q which of the following is a form of attack that prevents users from assessing normal services such as email or web server?
8. Q which IEEE standard defines the file wall technology?
9. . Q which type of memory transfers data
10. Q: Which type of video connector
11. Q. Which of the following can
12. Q, Which condition refer to a sudden

13. Q: What is the last step in the trouble shooting process?

14. Q which open source operating system is available on multiple hardware platform?

15. Q which registry file contains information about the hardware and software and computer system?

16. Q: what are the two advantages of SSID over magnetic hardware?

17. Q: Which 2 Optical Dr media store more than 5GB and can be re-written?

18. Q: which type of drive is used as external data storage

19. Q what statement is true about a high RAID 5 and RAID1?

20. Q which power management control was introduced prior to the advanced

21. Q: What do you do when you are unable to connect to home computer?

22. Q how do you secure a wireless network?

23. Q what is the name given to analyses as security

24. Q what is the first step in trouble shooting?
25. Q what do you do after a quick fix fail?
26. 29. Q what do you do first after customer giving you information?
27. Q what happened after you have solved the problem?
28. Q: A user cannot connect to the network using
29. Q:You locate a file on the server but cannot download it what do you do?
30. Q a user refuse your request to an email .
31. Q: a visiting consultant using a guest account
32. Q A customer reports that a backup that was started ……….
33. Q: You receive an error message that a computer will not lunch……..
34. Q: if the hard disk drive is making noise or morning about hard
35. Q what is the quickest way to install window XP
36. Q: After installing an updated graphics the screen

37. Q: You are unable to access one of the hard drive that has operating system

38. Q Which aspect of security include biometrics and door locks?

39. Q which practice is a minimum requirement securing network?

40. Q which item physically protects network media from damage and authorised access?

41. Q: Which type of lunch by hacker appearing to be trusted

42. Q: What is a safety concern that technician need to remember when working on CRT.?

43. Q what will affect choice of N/C in new site?

44. Q what should you not perform when dealing with computer repair to avoid ESD

45. Q how can the last known good configuration AGP= advanced graphic port.

46. Q: What happens if application lock up

47. Q the computer will no longer boot to windows and gives the invalid system error.
48. Q the computer will not finished loading Windows?
49. Q: Why do we need to implement preventive maintenance?
50. Q name few things that preventive maintenance consist of.
51. Q name few things that preventive maintenance consist of.
52. Q: Where do you find tools to use in a preventive measures?
53. Q name some windows utility that can be used in preventive?
54. Q name some window utilities to help with preventive measures.
55. Q explain Defrag
56. Q what and how to create window restore point?
57. Q what is ERD
58. Q name few backup media.
59. Q: What is security Key fob?
60. Q what is biometric device?
61. Q What is packets Firoz?
62. Q what is proxy firewall?

63. Q: What is proxy server?

64. Q what is hard were firewall?

65. Q what is VPN?

66. Q: What is CHKDSK?

67. Q how do you create window. Restore Points?

68. Q When should you

69. Q; What does Bios?

70. Q: what is Microsoft system preparation(SYSPREEP?

71. Q what is MISCONFIG?

72. Q: What does operating system provide the computer?

73. Q what is system file locations?

74. Q. What does network operating system A(NOS) contain?

75. Q: Give example of network operating system

76. Q what does the one attended installation do.

77. Q: What does the on attended installation in windows vista do.?

78. Q described device drive?

79. Q; Explain PnP

80. Q explain compatibility mode.

81. Q: What is HCL?

82. Q:When must a user perform a clean installation?

83. Q what is primary partition?

84. Q when does archived take place?

85. Q explain creation of image-based installation.

86. Q what does the computer use to boot up the system?

87. Q what is caching or storing?

88. Q how does investigation for a problem?

89. Q explain SFC.

90. Q explain BSOD Blue screen of death?.

91. Q how do you edit the boots configuration?

92. Q Which Windows operating system is capable of addressing up to 1128 GB of RAM.?

93. Q which two of these three steps should be performed to install windows XP service package

94. Q Which two Windows operating system can be upgraded to windows vista

95. Q what is the window Vista graphical pain that display and organizes small program such as clock games and web information?

96. Q: Which settings determines the order for which device are checked for an operating system when a computer boots?

97. Q which two conditions cause a computer keyboard to operate incorrectly?

98. Q: Which to statements described why a computer operating system would fail to start after a successful post?

99. Q In the installation of windows vista, what is meant by the phrase clean installation?

100. Q: what option are available if the customer installation type is selected?

101. Q what is the default desktop theme for a successful installation of window Vista business?

102. Q: Which three common tasks are performed during preventive maintenance?

103. Q In which to situation is it recommended to ask the customer to sign a liability form before attempting any kind of repair?

104. Q which type of question allows the customer to completely described the problem?

105. Q Which Windows application can be used to obtain details information about errors that have occurred in the system?

106. Q: Which Windows application can be used to obtain details information about errors that have occurred in the system

107. Q: A newly installed hard drive is not working well should the technician look to see if the drive is recognised by the system.

108. Q: What does operating system do.?

109. Q what does operating system provide?

110. Q: What is the roles of operating system?

111. Q how does the operating system communicate with the hardware?

112. Q: What is the name of the file structure created by operating system on hard drive?

113. Q: What is directly?

114. Q: what is SOP directories?

115. Q what is folders?

116. Q:How many types of users interface?

117. Q: what is mauled of operation?

118. Q what is UAC

119. Q: what is the significance of application program interface

120. Q: What are the characteristics of this top?

121. Q which window creative system combine both home and business users?

122. Q: What does the operative system does with the Programme install.?

123. Q what is the significance of API and application program interface name 2?

124. Q: What is direct X?

125. Q: what are the two common architecture used by CPU processor to process data?

126. Q; Name the two types of operative system?

127. Q; explain Spam.

128. Q what is blue tooth technology?

129. Q: What is printing writing?

130. Q what is FUSING?

131. Q: Explain in IMPACT printers

132. Q Name some advantage of an impact printers

133. Q what is NLQ?

134. Q: What is Piezoeledric

135. Q: What is the advantage of inkjet printer?

136. Q this advantage of an inkjet printer?

137. Q; What type of printers available?

138. Q:How do we measured speed of the printer?

139. Q: How do we measure the quality of the print?

140. Q Where can one find information about a printer

141. Q: What must one consider when buying a printer?

142. Q; How is serial data transfer.?

143. Q: What is the advantages of all in one devices. or printer?

144. Q: What is the disadvantages of all in one printer.?

145. Q what happens if a user is using different operating system?

146. Q how does the computer server get the new software?

147. .Q: What does flatbed scanner is useful.?

148. Q what are drum scanners use.?

149. Q how does printer problems occurred?

150. Q; Explain printer server.

151. Q how do printer's memory increase.?

152. Q: Explain scanning resolution.

153. Q: what is the best way to lift?

154. Q How do you connect a printer to your computer?

155. Q What is graphic device interface?.

156. Q; Described PDL?

157. Q how do you set a printer as a default?

158. Q what is IT8?

159. Q: how do you clean laser printer?.

160. Q: Explain ink jet printers.

161. Q how do you check the level of ink in the printer?.

162. Q how can you increase a printer function

163. Q how do you measure spanner resolution?

164. Q how do you adjust the colour calibration?.

165. Q:How does a printer create text

166. Q: what are the format images from the scan?

167. Q why is scanner collaboration important.?

168. Q how do you calibrate scan?.

169. Q:How do you start a new photocopy?.

170. Q how does develop of the printer.?

171. Q How is the image transfer?

172. Q: What is the final stage of photocopying.?

173. Q: How does impact printers operate?

174. Q: How many types of Impact printer.

175. Q: Which printer use continuous and has come on paper ability is impact printer and daisy wheel printers

176. Q; How does Dot Matrix printers work?

177. Q how do you calibrate printer?

178. Q; What's the name of the quality of dot-mix printer

179. Q what platen.?

180. Q: Explain inkjet printers?..

181. Q; how many types of ink jet printers?.

182. Q; Explain solid ink printer.

183. Q Describe thermal printers.

184. Q: How do you install print?

185. Q what is printer memory population?

186. Q: Which type of printing process uses solid sheets of ink that change directly to gas when the print head hit the ink?.

187. Q which the peripherals is used to convert up paper documents into electronic files.

188. Q a customer purchased the scanner

189. Q Which type of printer melts ink and

190. Q what technology is used by dot matrix printer?.

191. Q: What printer is used in library and Museum?.

192. Q how is the speed of a laser printer measured?.

193. Q what is an advantage of any net web printer over their local printer?.

194. Q a student on a window XP computer sent a print job to a newly installed printer that is connected to

195. Q how are electronic files produce?

196. Q what printer will provide carbon paper?

197. Q what are the printers selection criteria?.

198. Q; What RGB produced by Dot?

199. Q how does printer produce
    colours?.

200. Q what TCO, total cost of
    ownership?.

201. Q: what is compactible interface for
    scanners?.

202. Q described serial connection?.

203. Q: Described parallel connection?.

204. Q how is printer quality is
    measured?

205. Q: Name parallel printers port?.

206. Q: What pot is use for
    communication by a printer?.

207. Q what interface use parallel?.

208. Q what does USB do?.

209. Q which interface is fastest?.

210. Q; What connection for printer
    scanner to Internet?.

211. Q what do you need for infrared?

212. Q what benefit from blue tooth?

213. Q: What does Wi-Fi allow?.

214. Q described two types of Wi-Fi?.

215. Q how many steps to print one
    copy?.

216. Q explain cleaning for laser
    printers?

217. Q; Described condition?

218. Q; How many international standard paper for printing.?

219. Q: how does LCD screen operates?

220. Q what are the types of LCD?

221. Q what is DLP. Digital light processing?.

222. Q: How many sheets does the LP produce for image?.

223. Q: What thus pixels stand for?.

224. Q what is the meaning Dot. Pitch

225. Q what is refresh rate.

226. Q what is interlace?.

227. Q what is cathode?

228. Q what is aspect ratio?

229. Q what are system resources?.

230. Q name some system resources?

231. Q what is another name for network port?.

232. Q what port uses IEEE1284 with 8 bit

233. Q what standard cable is for printer?

234. Q how many devise can SCSI ports support?.

235. Q what is the maximum speed
    SCSI ports?

236. Q: what is the maximum length of
    SCSI for one device

237. Q if more than one computer what
    length is needed?

238. Q; What does HDMI function

239. Q how many pains(DV1)?.

240. Q how many pins VGA have.?

241. Q how many things S. Video have?

242. Q what is maximum length of
    network cable?.

243. Q: What is another name for fire
    wire?

244. Q what is firmware?

245. Q: How many device can fire wire
    IEEE take?

246. Q how many device and USB port
    support?

247. Q what is the speed of USB 1.1

248. Q what is the speed of USB two?

249. Q: what is capacity of CD optical?

250. Q what is the capacity of DVD?

251. Q What port has either DD-25 or
    transmits one data at a time

252. Q: What does GUI mean.

253. Q what is the image from camera and video store?

254. Q: what is barcode?

255. Q: What is Security dongle

256. : What is Firewall

257. Q: What is minimum computer security

258. Q: What is symmetric encryption?

259. Q: What is VPN?

260. Q: What is Lapping protection?

261. Q: What is Key fab

262. Q: What is proxy firewall?

263. Q: What is NT backup?

264. Q: What does proxy protect the computer.

265. Q: What is Antenna

266. Q: What is WPA OR WPA 2

267. Q: What is WRT300N

268. Q: What is DDos

269. Q: What is Spyware?

270. Q: What is Phishing

271. Q: WTLS is a special protocol

272. Q: What is Biometric

273. Q: What does WPA means.

274. Q: What are two levels of password?

275. Q; Describe Window Vista master boots

276. Q: What is Port 80

277. Q: How does virus does in Computer?

278. Q; How does Stealth viruses work?

279. Q: How worm works inflicting computer?

280. Q; Describe how Trojan works?

281. Q: Explain how Java works on computers

282. Q: What does DOS react on computer

283. Q; What does E mail bomb act dream?

284. Q; How does DDOS act on computer

285. Q: Describe how Span works on computer

286. Q How does social engineer behave?

287. Q: Describe how computer is protecting

288. Q: How can one guarantee that data on computer is saved?

289. Q Name other ways to prevent the computer being physically being stolen.

290. Q: How does Java scrip used to protect computer.

291. Q: What other ways can you prevent computers hackers

292. Q: What can be installed on computer by hackers without knowledge of the owner?

293. Q: What is Malware

294. Q: What is Phishing

295. Q: What is the important of good Pass word

296. Q: What is the rules of password

297. Q:How does (VPN) protect the computer data.

298. Q: Explain how WEP protect computer

299. Q: What are some Physical security
Physical security involves four interrelated aspects which include access,

300. Q: What security recommend for hardware?

301. Q: What do one use to protect
Secure tele-communication room

302. Q: What is available to protect
individual computer

303. Q: What application to protect the
hardware?

304. Q: What can be used to protect
operation system?

305. Q:Explain Asymmetric encryption

306. Q: Explain Symmetric encryption

307. Q: What is Hash and according?

308. Q: What is VPN

309. .Q; Name few Physical security?

310. Q: what is Smart card.

Chapter   24

Question and Answers

1. Q what is a common cause of error message "invalid system disc"

   A

   There is a non-bootable floppy disk or CD in the drive.

2. Q Name one type of PC card

   A

   Express card the PC express card has

3. Q; How many configuration?

   A

   34 to 54

4. Q: which power mode would you use on a laptop running window XP to minimize power consumption by reducing power to the hardware.

   A

   Hibernate.

5. Q which protocol maps known IP
    address to MAC address on a local
    network?

    A.

    ARP.

6. Q which of the following uses the network to
    duplicate its code to the host on a network
    often without any user intervention?

    A

    Worm

7. Q which of the following is a form of attack
    that prevents users from assessing normal
    services such as email or web server?

    A

    Denial of service

8. Q which IEEE standard defines the file wall
    technology?

    A

    1394.

9. Q which type of memory transfers data twice
as fast as S Drum and increase performance by
transferring data twice per cycle?

A

DDR SDRM.

10. Q: Which type of video connector has a 24pin or 29 pin female connector and provides compressed digital output to monitor?

A

ADVI

11.   Q. Which of the following can cause permanent to electrical company if you do not use proper tools and safety Presidium?

A

ESD.

12. Q, Which condition refer to a sudden and dramatic increase in voltage, which is usually because by lighting

A

SPIKE.

13. Q: What is the last step in the trouble shooting process?

A

close with the customer.

14. Q which open source operating system is available on multiple hardware platform?

A

LINUX.

15. Q which registry file contains information about the hardware and software and computer system?

A

HKEY-Local Machine.

16. Q: what are the two advantages of SSID over magnetic hardware?

A.

Access to data.

Reduce power storage.

17. Q: Which 2 Optical Dr media store more than 5GB and can be re-written?

A

BD-RE and DVD+-RW

18. Q: which type of drive is used as external data storage attaches using a seven pin

connector and has a maximum cable length of 2 meters?

A

eSATA.

19. Q what statement is true about a high RAID 5 and RAID1?

A.

RAID five takes more time to write.

20. Q which power management control was introduced prior to the advanced configuration and Power Interface?

A

advance power management APM.

21. Q: What do you do when you are unable to connect to home computer?

A.

The configure the SSID and any security setting manually.

22. Q how do you secure a wireless network?

A

Change the defaults administrative password for all access points use

MAC filtering

23. Q what is the name given to analyses as
security threats and determine the
appropriate method to protect the assets
and for large repair.

A

trouble shooting.

24. Q what is the first step in trouble shooting?

A

gather information from use signs and
symptoms.

25. Q what do you do after a quick fix fail?

A

obtain course on disc management or event.

26. 29. Q what do you do first after customer
giving you information?

A.

Try quick fit.

27. Q what happened after you have solved the
problem?

A.

Write in customer Journal and explain the
solution with the user.

28. Q: A user cannot connect to the network
    using a wireless router even after the proper
    security key has been installed what do you
    do?

    A

    verified that the users MAC address is listed
    in the top MAC address in the filter table

29. Q:You locate a file on the server but cannot
    download it what do you do?

    A

    change the use so permission on this file
    from read only to read and execute.

30. Q a user refuse your request to an email . To
    give you the student pass word and ID
    number

    A.

    Inform the user that there was no such
    request, run him against phishing

31. Q: a visiting consultant using a guest account
    cannot assess needed files what would you
    do?

A

Grant him passes to the files for the duration of the visit when the consultant leaves is able the account.

32. Q A customer reports that a backup that was started the night before is still going on how would you advise?

A

Advise the customer to implement a different type of backup that saves time.

Questions and answers on operating system.

33. Q: You receive an error message that a computer will not lunch because the required service is not running what would you do

A

note the name of the service in the error message in the computer journal then restart the service.

34. Q: if the hard disk drive is making noise or morning about hard drive becoming full what is the solution.

A

Try the disc clean-up utility or defragmentation to delete temporary files.

35. Q what is the quickest way to install window XP on 100 computers in an office during the weekend?

A

Use one of the automated installation solution.

36. Q: After installing an updated graphics the screen goes blank how do you solve it?

A.

The new driver may be bad, boot the computer in the VGA mode and use rollback to restore the previous driver

37. Q: You are unable to access one of the hard drive that has operating system?

A

check that boot.ini is not corrupt and make sure it is correct.

38. Q Which aspect of security include biometrics and door locks?

A

securing access to facilities.

39. Q which practice is a minimum requirement securing network?

A

creating secure login information for all users.

40. Q which item physically protects network media from damage and authorised access?

A

conduit.

41. Q: Which type of lunch by hacker appearing to be trusted organisation and send up email to trick the user into providing confidential information?

A:

Phishing

42. Q: What is a safety concern that technician need to remember when working on CRT.?

A

risk of electrical shock.

43. Q what will affect choice of N/C in new site?

A

availability of expansion slot, next work

protocols used in the new location.

44. Q what should you not perform when dealing

with computer repair to avoid ESD?

A

make sure the room is carpeted. The room is

serviced is cool and dry.

45. Q how can the last known good configuration

AGP= advanced graphic port.

A

VRM= voltage regulator model in the

motherboard.

46. Q: What happens if application lock up

A

If application lock up all computer displays

frequent error message what do you do.

 change RAM

option   be accessed.

press F8 to access the advance boot option.

47. Q the computer displays desktop in 16colourVGA moat after getting the video driver?

A use the rollback driver option to remove the new video driver. Remove any unnecessary program from the start to tab and reboots the computer

48. Q the computer will no longer boot to windows and gives the invalid system error.

A

remove any floppies and CDs run from the computer and verified that the hard drive is set as a bootable device in the Bios set up

49. Q the computer will not finished loading Windows?

A

Boot the computer in safe mode and install in the recently installed application

50. Q: Why do we need to implement preventive maintenance?

A to decrease down time.

To improve performance.

To improve reliability.

To decrease repair cost.

51. Q name few things that preventive maintenance consist of.

A; Claiming, inspecting, and doing manor repairs.

52. Q: Where do you find tools to use in a preventive measures?

A

there are physical tools and diagnostic other can be loaded from the operative system onto the hard disk.

53. Q name some windows utility that can be used in preventive?

A

The DOS AT command to launch task. and specific time using a graphic user's interface By following the former starts then run them and then type AT1 at command line.

54. Q name some window utilities to help with preventive measures.

A

scan disk or CHKDSK are used to check the integrity of files and folders, the high disc for physical errors.

55. Q explain Defrag

A

it means gather files which are spread all over the place and arranged them in order so that the files can be found and great space.
It helps to provide more space and increase the speed of the computer as is easier for the computer to locate files.

56. Q what and how to create window restore point?

A

this is how the window XP create an image at the current computer settings so that when there is a problem and some files missing, windows can roll back to a previous configuration
It is strongly advisable to create a restore points prowl to bits for repair you do this by following procedure

starts then choosing all Programme and then choose accessories and then choose system then tools then system restore.

57. Q what is ERD

A:

it stand for emergency repair disk. Window 2000 can create ERD and self-critical boots files and configuration information.

58. Q name few backup media.

A

tape drive use for data backup on a network. The digital audio tape DAT used to store data in the digital data storage DSS format. DLT digital linear tape this offer high capacity and high-speed tape backup, combability . USB flash memory store much more data than floppy disk

59. Q: What is security Key fob?

A

Is a small device that resembles the ornament on the key using it's for a small radio system that communicates with the computer over a short range. The computer must detect the signal before it will accept a username and password.

60. Q what is biometric device?

A

This measures and physical, characteristic of the user, such as fingerprints or patterns of the iris in the eye. A firewall should be used in addition.

61. Q What is packets Firoz?

A:

up this is a set of rules that allows or denies traffic based on some criteria such as IP address, protocols, or ports use

62. Q what is proxy firewall?

A

This is a firewall installed on proxy server, that inspects all traffic allows or denies packets based on config rate rules, up

63. Q: What is proxy server?

A

Is a server that relay between a client and a is to destination server on the Internet.

64. Q what is hard were firewall?

A

Is a physical filtering component that inspect data packets from the network before its rich the computer and other devices on the network. These are freestanding units that does not use the resources of the computers. It is protecting so there is no impact on processing performance.

65. Q what is VPN?

A

this uses secure protocols to encrypt and to secure data as if it was travelling in the private corporate. Lan even though the data actually over any networks or intranets the secure data pipelines between points in the VPN are called secure tunnel

66. Q: What is CHKDSK?

A.

this checks the integrity of files and folders and scan the hard disk surfaces for physical perils.

67. Q how do you create window. Restore Points?

A:

Restore points can create an image of current computer settings called a restore point then if the computer crashes or and have dates causes the system problems the computer and rollback to a previous configuration always create and restore point before updating or replacing the computer system.

68. Q When should you?

A.

Restore points should be created at the following times stop

when an application is installed

when a driver is installed.

Backup tools allows the recovery of data.

69. Q; What does Bios?

A.

This boot the computer using the first drive that contains an operating system once the driver with the operating system is located, the BIOS locate the master boots records(MBR) which intends locate the operating system boots loader for window XP the goods loader is called NT loader NTLDR. Prop

70. Q: what is Microsoft system preparation(SYSPREEP?

A:

This is to install and configure it the same operating system on multiple computers.

71. Q what is MISCONFIG?

A.

the Misconfigure command bring up the system configuration utility that performs and diagnostic procedures on the windows starts up file. You must be logged on with administrators permission to complete the troubleshooting Procedure. MISCONFIG should be used when the computer boots but will not load Windows operating system correctly

72. Q: What does operating system provide the computer?

A

An operating system provide the following operational and organisation capabilities include

and breached between the hardware and applications.

It creates a file system to store data.

it manages applications.

73. Q: what is system file locations?

A

when the Windows operating system is in store, all of the files that are used to run the computer are located in the folder c;/WINNT/SYSTEM32 for windows 2000 and ?windows/system32 for windows XP and Windows vista.

74. Q. What does network operating system A(NOS) contain?

A

It contains additional features to increase functionality and manageably in network management

75. Q: Give example of network operating system

A

Example of network operating system are

Windows 2000 server

Windows 2003 server

window 2010 server

UNIX

LINUX

Novell Netware

Mess OSX

The NOS let work operating system is designed to provide network resources to clients

76. Q what does the one attended installation do.

A

The one attended installation in window XP using an unattended.txt answer file is the easiest customer installation method to perform on a network environment.

77. Q: What does the on attended installation in windows vista do.?

A

Two customise a standard windows vista installation the SIM or system image manager is used to create the setup answer file. The windows SIM allows to perform the following operations.

Create and Unattended answer file.

Update and on attended answer file.

I packages such as applications or drivers and on attended answer file.

AIK

the windows sim is part of the Windows automatic installation kit and can be downloaded from the Microsoft website..

78. Q described device drive?

A

device drive is a small program written by the hardware manufacture and supply with the hardware component, when the hardware drive or devise is installed, the device driver is also installed, allowing the operative system to communicate with the hardware components

79. Q; Explain PnP

A

The process of assigning system resources and installing drivers can be performed with plug and play. All the modern operating system are PnP compatible,

80. Q explain compatibility mode.

A

Compatibility mode can create the proper environment or versions of the operating system to allow the application to run as if it is in the intended environment. Up

81. Q: What is HCL?

A.

Most operating system have a hardware capability list (CCL) that can be found on the manufacturers website.

82. Q:When must a user perform a clean installation?

A

when a computer is passed from one employee to another.

When the operating system is corrupted.

When a new replacement hard drive is in store in a computer.

83. Q what is primary partition?

A

This is usually the first partition and cannot
be subdivided into smaller section there can
be up to 4 partitions per hard drive.

84. Q when does archived take place?

A

File will be archived the next time that the disc
is backed

85. Q explain creation of image-based installation.

A

when performing image-based installation,
begins by completely configuring one
computer to an operational state. Next run
Sysprep to prepare the system for imaging. At
third party drive imaging application prepares
an image of the completed computer which
can be burned onto a CD or DVD
This image can then be copied onto
computers with, compatible hardware access
layers (HALs). Two complete the installation
of multiple computers.

86. Q what does the computer use to boot up the
system?

A

The computing system uses the active partition to boot up the system. The active partition must be a primary partition. C;/drive is the active partition and contains the boots and system files

87. Q what is caching or storing?

A

Internet files is a future of the web browser that is used to speed up the process of assessing previously visited website has the are stalled in the temporary files and need frequently dealing. with.

88. Q how does investigation for a problem?

A

To investigate the problem and restore the settings in window XP, Reboot the computer during the boot phase, press the F8 key. Enter the boot options, you can then select rollback driver from the properties.

89. Q explain SFC.

A

The system file checker allows you to check all of the protected system files, such as Kvm/386.exe and replace them with known good version if they have become corrupted or deleted

90. Q explain BSOD Blue screen of death?.

A

The event log and other diagnostic utilities are available to research and stop Errol on BSOD. The stop Errol is a hardware and software malfunction that causes the system to lock up. This type of Errol is known has blue screen of death usually caused by Advice drive, error.

91. Q how do you edit the boots configuration?

A

To edit the boots configuration data in Windows vista, use the bcd.exe Edits.exe command line tool to assess the bcdedit. tool. In window Vista press start then all programs then accessories than right click the command prompt then run as administrator then continue then type bcdedit.

92. Q Which Windows operating system is capable of addressing up to 1128 GB of RAM.?

A

window vista(64)

93. Q which two of these three steps should be performed to install windows XP service package

A

Download important habit to windows vista

94. Q Which two Windows operating system can be upgraded to windows vista

A

Window 2000 and window and T Window XP to window Vista?

95. Q what is the window Vista graphical pain that display and organizes small program such as clock games and web information?

A

Side bar.

96. Q: Which settings determines the order for which device are checked for an operating system when a computer boots?

A

The BIOS boot device certain which
Microsoft, used direct X component?

97. Q which two conditions cause a computer
keyboard to operate incorrectly?
A
The keyboard has a hardware fault
The cable is damaged or connected
incorrectly.

98. Q: Which to statements described why a
computer operating system would fail to start
after a successful post?
A
The master boot record is corrupt.
The boot drive contains non-bootable media

99. Q In the installation of windows vista, what is
meant by the phrase clean installation?
A
An installation that does not preserve any
information from previous installation
In the window XP operating system to
Windows Vista,

100.   Q: what option are available if the customer installation type is selected?

A

Advance options are made available, such as creating a new partition for the installation.

101. Q what is the default desktop theme for a successful installation of window Vista business?

A

AERO

102. Q: Which three common tasks are performed during preventive maintenance?

A

Check

103. Q In which to situation is it recommended to ask the customer to sign a liability form before attempting any kind of repair?

A

The technician is unable to back up the customer information.

The customer is unable to provide a backup

104.   Q which type of question allows the customer to completely described the problem?

A

Open-ended question.

105.   Q Which Windows application can be used to obtain details information about errors that have occurred in the system?

A

check and secure loose cables.
Clean the mouse and keyboard.
Upgrade the drivers.

106.   Q: Which Windows application can be used to obtain details information about errors that have occurred in the system

A

event viewer.

107. Q: A newly installed hard drive is not working well should the technician look to see if the drive is recognised by the system.

A . BIOS

108. Q: What does operating system do.?

A

It controls almost all function on the computer.

109. Q what does operating system provide?

A

It provide interface for into reaction between useless applicants and hardware. It also puts the system.

110. Q: What is the roles of operating system?

A

It controls hardware assets, manage files and folders, provide user interface, manage applications.

111. Q how does the operating system communicate with the hardware?

A

The operating system install a device driver which is a program into their hardware which allows the operating system to communicate with the hardware.

112. Q: What is the name of the file structure created by operating system on hard drive?

A

File is blocked of related data giving single men.

113. Q: What is directly?

A

Programme and data files

114. Q: what is SOP directories?

A

When directories kept inside directory.

115. Q what is folders?

A

Directories known as folders and sub directory known as sub folders.

116. Q:How many types of users interface?

A

There are two namely command line interface CLI and graphical user interface GUI

117. Q: what is mauled of operation?

A

It's capabilities of the CPU you and the operating environment

118. Q what is UAC

A:

it allows an application to be run if the user does not have the required administrative privilege

119. Q: what is the significance of application program interface

A.

Is guidelines used by programs to ensure the Programme is Cooper ability with operational system top for small office or home office, and network operation system which serves multiple users.

120. Q: What are the characteristics of this top?

A

support as single user, runs single user, application, share files and folders on small network with limited security.

121.   Q which window creative system combine both home and business users?

A

Windows vista utilities

122.   Q: What does the operative system does with the Programme install.?

A

It notes it on to run and make sure it has adequate system resources.

123.   Q what is the significance of API and application program interface name 2?

A

Guidelines used by programs to ensure the Programme is compellable with operating system.

It's open graphic library cross platform standard for multimedia graphics.

124.   Q: What is direct X?

A

Is collection of application program interface relating to multimedia tasks for Microsoft.

125.   Q: what are the two common architecture used by CPU processor to process data?

A

X86(32architecture uses CISC current next instructions set computer this use fewer registry.

X64 964BIT ARCHITECTURE use more register

126.   Q; Name the two types of operative system?

A

Small office home office(SOHO)

let's work operate tooth system serve multiple uses(NOS) .is us for more complex instruction

127.   Q; explain Spam.

A

Spam is used as a method of advertising; however it can be used to send harmful links or deceptive content. When used as an attack method, spam may include links to an infected website or an attachment, also lead you to advertising sites. These windows are

called pop-ups. Many antivirus and email
software programs automatically detect and
remove spam from email box.

PRINTING SCANNING

128.   Q what is blue tooth technology?
A
A group tooth technology uses an online
sense radio for
Frequency for short range communication.

129.   Q: What is printing writing?
A
Writing is process involves scanning the
photosensitive drum with laser beam.

130.   Q what is FUSING?
A
It is the last process to print information onto
a single sheet of paper.

131.   Q: Explain in IMPACT printers.
A

Impact printers are very basic printers Dot-matrix and daisy wheel are example of impact printers.

132.   Q Name some advantage of an impact printers.

A

Noisy

No resolution graphics

Ltd colour capability

133.   Q what is NLQ?

A

The highest quality of print that is produced by the dot. matrix printers is referred to as near letter quality.

134.   Q: What is Piezoeledric

A

Piezoeledric are located in the ink reservoir at the back of each nozzle.

135.   Q: What is the advantage of inkjet printer?

A

Advantage of an inkjet printer.

A low cost

High resolution.

136.   Q this advantage of an inkjet printer?

A

nozzle are prone to clogging

ink cartridges are expensive.

Ink is weight of the printing.

137. Q; What type of printers available?

A

Printer available today are usually either

Laser printer or using electrophotographic

technology. Or inkjet printers using electoral

tonic spray.

138. Q:How do we measured speed of the

   printer?

A

The speed of a printer is measured in page

per minute (ppm)

139. Q: How do we measure the quality of the

   print?

A

The quality of printing is measured in dots per

inch(dpi) the more dpi the high the resolutions

When the resolution is higher text and image are usually clearer. To produce the best high-resolution image you should use both high quality ink or toner and high-quality paper.

140.   Q Where can one find information about a printer?

A

Information is found in the model or the manufacturers website.

141.   Q: What must one consider when buying a printer?

A

Consider the costs when selecting hardware, when by a printer, there is more than just the initial costs of the printer to consider.
The total costs of ownership (TCO) includes a number of factors which is known as total cost of ownership.

142.   Q; How is serial data transfer.?

A

The data transfer is the movement of single bits of information in a single cycle. A serial connection can be used for. Metrix printers because the printer do not require high speed data transfer

.

143. Q: What is the advantages of all in one devices. or printer?

A

all devices are built in scanner, fax, printer.
Low cost.
Upgrades are easier soft where is design for all devices
connection and setup is easy one port.

144. Q: What is the disadvantages of all in one printer.?

A

Dot modular if one device breaks or devices may not be operational.
Not design for heavy use.

145. Q what happens if a user is using different operating system?

A

If you so are you saying different operating system than the computer that is hosting the share printer windows can automatically download the correct driver to for the new user.

146.   Q how does the computer server get the new software?

A

A quick the additional drivers button to select operative system that the other uses may be using. But if all of the order uses are also using the same windows operating system you do not need to click the additional drivers button.

147.   .Q: What does flatbed scanner is useful.?

A.

They are often used to scan books and photographs for archiving.

148.   Q what are drum scanners use.?

A

They produce a high-quality transfer of an image; many drum scanners are still in use for high and reproductions such as achieving photographs in the museums..

149.   Q how does printer problems occurred?

A

A print problems can result from a combination of hardware, software, and network issues.

150. Q; Explain printer server.

A

Printer server needs to have resources available to meet the requests of print clients. Powerful processor, adequate hard drive space, adequate memory.

151. Q how do printer's memory increase.?

A

Upgrading the kinks memory increases the printing speed and harness complex print jobs performance. All printers have RAM the added memory helps with task such as job buffering, page creation, improve photo printing and graphics.

152. Q: Explain scanning resolution.

A.

Scanning resolution affects the size of the output file,
Medium resolution images are normally used for laser prints.

In commercial printing a higher resolution is the best setting low resolution means small file size high resolution means large file size.

153.   Q: what is the best way to lift?

A.

always lift equipment by using the strength in your legs and knees, not your back.

154.   Q How do you connect a printer to your computer?

A

When you connect a new printer device to a computer, Windows locate and installs a default driver by using(PnP) plug and play.

155.   Q What is graphic device interface?.

A

Graphic device interface is a window complement that manages how graphical image are transmitted to output devices. Works by converting images to a bit map that uses the computer instead of the printer to transfer the images.

PDL

156. Q; Described PDL?

A

Page description language is a type of cold
that describes the appearance of the
documents in a language that a printer can
understand software application uses PDLs
27 what you see is what you get(WY51NYG)
images to the printer.

157. Q how do you set a printer as a default?
A
Start then Control Panel then printers and
faxes right click the printer's and choose to set
as before. Printer.

158. Q what is IT8?
A
To ensure calibration compare the output of
the IT8 target stop I just the printer colour
settings too much the I T8 target the next time
your prints or scan an image the colour should
much the target.

159. Q: how do you clean laser printer?.
A

When cleaning a laser printer, use a special designed vacuum cleaner to pick up toner particles. Use only vacuum cleaner with HEPA filtration HEPA filtration catches microscopic particles within the filters

160. Q: Explain ink jet printers.

A

when an inkjet printer produces blank pages the ink cartridges may be empty. Laser printers however do not produce blank pages but do begin to print very Poor quality print out most inkjet printer provide a utility that show ink level in each cartridge, some printers have screen or LED light when ink surprise are low.

161. Q how do you check the level of ink in the printer?.

A

method for checking ink level is to look at the page counter inside the printer or the printer software to determine how many pages have been printed. Because ink cartridge normally tells how many prints you could get out of the.

162. Q how can you increase a printer function

A

update the drivers and firewall to fix problems
and increase functionality

163.   Q how do you measure spanner
    resolution?

A

resolution of the scanner is measured dpi (dot
per inch) higher dot the better the picture
images and TEXT.

164. Q how do you adjust the colour
    calibration?.

A

To I just colour calibration go to certain too much
the colour on screen to the colours on the printer
sheet.

165.   Q:How does a printer create text

A

OCR optical character recognition allows colour
to create text document

166. Q: what are the format images from the scan?

A

Images from the scanner convert RGB to JPEG,TIFF,BMP,PNG.

167. Q why is scanner collaboration important.?

A

 scanner colour collaboration between devices is important helps to see true colour

168. Q how do you calibrate scan?.

 A

 scan a graphic that contain specific colours. A calibration application install on the computer, compare the outputs of the scanner against the sample of the graphic.

169. Q:How do you start a new photocopy?.

 A

 put the sheet to be copied on the grass as the drum moves the light create and laser beam which scan the paper onto the photo sensitive drum (-100 Vol up DC) creating invisible latent image on the drum.

170. Q how does develop of the printer.?
A developing; the taller which is now negative charge make of plastic and metal particle from the control blade is applied to the latent image on the positive charge drum.

171. Q How is the image transfer?
A

The latent image with the toner is then transferred onto paper which is positive charge whilst drum is negative charge, the drum with toner attract the positive paper to create the latent image to be visible this transfer is called secondary corona.

172. Q: What is the final stage of photocopying.?
A

The final stage is call fusing the paper with wet toner move between heated roller and pressure roller which dry the toner or print and lose toner melted and fused with the fibers in the paper, the finished paper is warm and move to the out tray.

Impact printers.

173. Q: How does impact printers operate?

A

Print heads strike the ink ribbon so that the characters are imprints on paper and it can have come on paper.

174. Q: How many types of Impact printer.

A

There are two types. metrics and daisy wheel.

175. Q: Which printer use continuous and has come on paper ability is impact printer and daisy wheel printers

A

Daisey Wheel
As the wheel(with character alphabets, numbers etc.) rotate an electromechanical hammer pushes up required character into the ink ribbon, striking the paper to print.

176. Q; How does Dot Matrix printers work?

A

The head contain pin with electromagnets which pushes forward out the ribbon to create characters on paper

177. Q how do you calibrate printer?

A

Adjust it at the setting.

178. Q; What's the name of the quality of dot-mix printer

A:

the highest quality of print Dot produced by-MIX is refer as near letter quality.

179. Q what platen.?

A.

Is a large roller that applied pressure to keep paper from slippery in dot-matrix.

180. Q: Explain inkjet printers?..

A

The ink cartridge spray ink onto a page through tiny holes called in jet nozzle.

181. Q; how many types of ink jet printers?.

A

there are two types firmer which is a steam
from chamber force ink through nozzles to
the paper.

Piezoelectric crystals vibrating of the crystals
control the flow through nozzles to the paper

182. Q; Explain solid ink printer.

A

The printer melt solid ink and spray through
nozzles onto drum which then transfer onto
the paper.

183. Q Describe thermal printers.

A

Thermal printers uses roles of paper
Dye-sublimation printers the process of
printer used solid sheet of ink from side solid
is sublimation the head is passes cyan,
magenta, yellow, and clear overcoat
up(CMYO)

184. Q: How do you install print?

A

Manufacturers website for our date the drive then download and on zip then install either automatic or manual then test by multiple prints.

185. Q what is printer memory population?

A

Is how many memory slots they are in the printer

186. Q: Which type of printing process uses solid sheets of ink that change directly to gas when the print head hit the ink?.

A

Dye sublimation.

187. Q which the peripherals is used to convert up paper documents into electronic files.

A

Scanners

188. Q a customer purchased the scanner shown in the traffic and this covers that it is limited to converting hard copy data into electronic images. Which type of scanner as the customer pages?.

A

flatbed.

189. Q Which type of printer melts ink and sprays it through and nozzle onto the drum to transfer an image onto paper?

A

Solid ink.

190. Q what technology is used by dot matrix printer?.

A

impact.

191. Q: What printer is used in library and Museum?.

A

rum scanner.

192. Q how is the speed of a laser printer measured?.

A.

pages pair minutes.

193. Q what is an advantage of any net web printer over their local printer?.

A.

it is used by multiple people.

194. Q a student on a window XP computer
sent a print job to a newly installed printer
that is connected to Elkhorn computer.
However the print job feels. Which to can be
used to verify the configuration of the port
that the printer is on?.

The reports tab of printer properties.

195. Q how are electronic files produce?

A

Electronic files are produced by flat bets
scanners it convert paper document to electronic
files.

196. Q what printer will provide carbon paper?

A

Dot matrix using impact technology.

197. Q what are the printers selection criteria?.

A

capacity, speed, colour, quality, reliability.

198. Q; What RGB produced by Dot?

A

red green and blue.

199. Q how does printer produce colours?.

A

Printer produce colours using subtractive mixing. Hi DPI will give higher quality need high quality ink or toner and paper high quality paper give high resolution.

200. Q what TCO, total cost of ownership?.

A

Initial purchase price, cost of supplies paper and ink, price per page, maintenance costs, warranty cost.

201. Q: what is compactible interface for scanners?.

A

Compactible interface for computers and scanners are parallel USB and wireless interface ports plus SCSI.

202. Q described serial connection?.

A

serial connection is slow, and it transfers single bits of information at the time and is used by dot matrix.

203. Q: Described parallel connection?.

A

Parallel connection is faster as it is transfer
multiple information in a single cycle.

204. Q how is printer quality is measured?

A.

Printer quality is measured in dots per inch DPI.

205. Q: Name parallel printers port?.

A

Current standard for parallel printer ports
includeIEEE1284 two modes within IEEE1284
which then produce EPP and Hans parallel
ports.

206. Q: What pot is use for communication by
a printer?.

A

ECP enhance capabilities port allows by
directional communication.

207. Q what interface use parallel?.

A

SCSI small computer system Interface

208. Q what does USB do?.

A

 USB ports is very fast and you SB support
PnP resorting that the computer detects the
device immediately

209. Q which interface is fastest?.

A.

FireWire interface also known as IEEE1394 i
link is the fastest and did provide block and
socket connection for 63 devices and
transfer rate over 400 MBS.

210. Q; What connection for printer scanner to
Internet?.

A

Ethernet (RJ-45)
Wireless (infrared;-Bluetooth and wireless.
Fidelity Wi-Fi technology.

211. Q what do you need for infrared?

A

you need transmitters for both hands
maximum of 12 feet.

212. Q what benefit from blue tooth?

A

Bluetooth adapter allows printers to be connected.

213. Q: What does Wi-Fi allow?.

A

 Wi-Fi allows connection to a computer network without using cable

214. Q described two types of Wi-Fi?.

A.

 802.11b transfer data at the rate of 11Mbps
802.11g transfer data at the rate of 54mbps
802.11g products are backwards compatible with 802.11
Laser printing.

215. Q how many steps to print one copy?.

A

 six
cleaning, conditioning, writing, developing, transferring fusing.
CCWDTF cleaning continuous care will delay trouble for ever

216. Q explain cleaning for laser printers?

A

remaining Donna after strong with Ghana
has been separated from paper on the drum
is removed either by printer rates to scrap
from drum, high-voltage, wire in the printer,
remove excess toner, the excess falls to
container.

217. Q; Described condition?

A

condition involve removing previous latent
image and condition of prepared the drum for
the next copy. This is done by special wire or
grind or 600 DC, then primary CORONA or a
ruler that receive 600 DC vote and negative
then the drum. This process is conditional
roller

218. Q; How many international standard
paper for printing.?

A

There are eight international standard paper
size rating from A0 To A8

A0 is the largest size, its size is exactly half the size of the one before it for example A1 is half the size of A0,AZ is half the size of A1 and so on.

The word default just means the original setting before you change it.

Auto fit is the: with for the hall table anyone go.

Left indent, handing indent, first line indents, right indent, Markers.

When there is only one operator your work from left to right, performing each calculator intense.

However when you mix operators the rule is to multiply and divide fast, then do any additional or subtraction.

If a calculator requires you to break the rule, such as at first and then multiply you use brackets to show which part calculator first How does CRT cathode screen operates?

A red green and blue electrons move back and forth on coated phosphorus screen

219.   Q: how does LCD screen operates?

A

there are two polarizing filters with liquid crystals solution between them, light pass or not pass through this electronic current.

220. Q what are the types of LCD?

A

 Active matrix, TFT, thin film transmitter, passive matrix.

221. Q what is DLP. Digital light processing?.

A.

is used in projectors spinning colour wheel with digital microprocessor device DMD.

222. Q: How many sheets does the LP produce for image?.

A

1024 sheets grey between white and black.

223. Q: What thus pixels stand for?.

A

picture element.

224. Q what is the meaning Dot. Pitch

A

Is the distance between pixels on screen

225. Q what is refresh rate.

A:

The rate of how often per second the image is rebuilt.

226.   Q what is interlace?.

A

when this can monitor by scanning image.

227.   Q what is cathode?

A

is non-interlace.

228.   Q what is aspect ratio?

A

Is horizontal to vertical 4,3 the view area of monitor

229.   Q what are system resources?.

A

To communicate between CP you and other components.

230.   Q name some system resources?

A

1/0 ports address, IRQ,DMA (direct memory address) 65535 1/o in computer.

231. Q what is another name for network port?.

A

RJ-45

232. Q what port uses IEEE1284 with 8 bit

A; Parallel port.

233. Q what standard cable is for printer?

A

type B 36 Centronics orc 36 pin Highspeed

234. Q how many devise can SCSI ports
support?.
A 15.

235. Q what is the maximum speed SCSI
ports?
A Excess of 320Mbps

236. Q: what is the maximum length of SCSI
for one device
A
80 feet.

237. Q if more than one computer what length
is needed?

A

40 feet

238. Q; What does HDMI function?

A

provide digital video and digital audio.

239. Q how many pains(DV1)?.

A

24 female or 29 female.

240. Q how many pins VGA have.?

A

15, three roles of three.

241. Q how many things S. Video have?

A

for things

242. Q what is maximum length of network
cable?.

100 m or 328 feet.

243. Q: What is another name for fire wire?

A

   i. Link

244. Q what is firmware?

   A

   soft while in the ROM

245. Q: How many device can fire wire IEEE take?

   A 63

246. Q how many device and USB port support?

   A

   127.

247. Q what is the speed of USB 1.1

   A

   1.5mbp-- 12mbps

248. Q what is the speed of USB two?

   A

   fall hundred 480 MBP

249. Q: what is capacity of CD optical?

   A

700 MB.

250. Q what is the capacity of DVD?

A

8.5 GBB9

251. Q What port has either DD-25 or

transmits one data at a time

A.

Serial

252. Q: What does GUI mean.

A

graphical user interface.

253. Q what is the image from camera and

video store?

A

A file

254. Q: what is barcode?

A

PC means "Universal Product Code." UPCs

are barcode symbols that manufacturers use

to identify their products electronically. This

lets those products be digitally scanned and

tracked. Each UPC consists of a series of digitally readable bars plus numbers that people can verify.

Microsoft hardware
 compatibility list,
OS (Operating System)

Microsoft hardware compatibility list
is supported by Microsoft operating systems.
A security policy must be enforced and
followed by all employees to be effective.
For physical threats to security are access,
data, infrastructure, and the computer itself.

255.   Q: What is Security dongle
        A
This is sure that the system locks if the user
and laptop are separated.

256.   Q: What is Firewall
        A
Firewall is built into window XP.

Inclusion detection system IDS monitor and report and exchanges on program code and on usual network activities.

Application and all OS (Operating system) patches.
Update, repair, regularly.

257. Q: What is minimum computer security

A

Antivirus and Anti-malware updates operation system with the latest patches and use firewall.

258. Q: What is symmetric encryption?

A

As symmetric encryption this required two keys sender have privately and the receiver key is public. Needed to code and on code

.

259. Q: What is VPN?

A

VPN.; Virtual private network this uses encryption to secure data. The secure data pipeline between the two points is called secure tunnels.

260. Q: What is Lapping protection?

A

Over lapping protection or two factor security.

this works by using two different techniques to protect assets example password and biometric or smartcard.

Data protection security

261. Q: What is Key fab

Key fab computer signal before grant access. Smart card and bowel metric is also useful for this

262. Q: What is proxy firewall?

A

if any individual or group is denying permissions to a network share, this denying overriding any of the permission given this means even the administrator will be denied

263. Q: What is NT backup?

A.

NT backup this is from command line and is for backup, but it cannot be used to restore

file for all normal incremental, differential, daily,
restore utility wizard files with extension bkf can be save on to hard drive, DVD, or any storage.

264. Q: What does proxy protect the computer.

A

It is inspect all traffic and allows or denies packets based on configured rules. Proxy acts as a gateway that protects computers inside the net.

265. Q: What is Antenna

A

Antenna influence where signal can be review receive. You must always change the default username and password of all wireless device to avoid other people getting access.

266. Q: What is WPA OR WPA 2

A

WPA 2 is improve version of WPA it can be enabled with password authentication which is personal or server authentication which is enterprise and these give it the strongest security and is normally used by governments. WPA OR WPA 2 is stronger than SSID up. Ipconfig/all=Mac address filtering.

267. Q: What is WRT300N

A

Firewall can be configured to block ports. WRT300N wireless router is also a hardware firewall, it allows traffic open and traffic originate from inside your network.

268. Q: What is DDos

A

DDos attack are resorts from many hosts participate in a coordinated attack.

269. Q: What is Spyware?

A

Spyware is a computer security threats that can be installed to somebody computer without the knowledge of the user. This will enable the installer to monitor the activities of that computer.

270. Q: What is Phishing

A

Phishing: is as security threats that uses you may and give an appearance to be from legitimate sender, may then ask the email recipient to visit a specific website to enter confidential information.

The best way to secure a wireless network is to change the default administrator password for all access points and to use MAC filtering.

271. Q: WTLS is a special protocol

A

When a wireless network is configured with WEP encryption all users have configured their computers for the WEP encryption . WTLS is a special protocol designed to provide security for W a P devices and bandwidth to be used efficiently.

If one take Internal Hard drive from a computer and reuse the same hard drive in another computer within same organisation you must reformat and reload an operating system on the drive.

272. Q: What is Biometric

A

Biometric is a physical characteristics for authentication.

Trusted platform model is a security specialise chip install in motherboard for authentication for hard and software.

273.   Q: What does WPA means.

   A

WPA means Wi-fi protected access.

Users must always set virus protection software to scan removable media when data is accessed by prohibited the use of removable media or network computer.

A computer user may receive 100/1000 of junk email every day. The course of this is possible the network is not providing detection or protection. The best solution is to filter out you may from the centres at the email server.

274.   Q: What are two levels of password?

A

You can have two level of password protection which are BIOS and Login .

Backup and restore centre in the computer is to use to manage backup and restoration of files on window

275.   Q; Describe Window Vista master boots

A

If virus damage the master boots record Errol loading operating system will be displayed
To provide minimum level of security to the access point, the default username and access point is powered on

Firewall in window Vista operating system can be managed manually by permitting or allowing specific ports

Ports forwarding is option in the firewall that provide a way to limit traffic based on a specific protocol for an indefinite period time.

276.   Q: What is Port 80

A

Port 80 must be open on firewall so that any computer can access webpages on the Internet
Great secure login information for all users is good practice to provide a maximum-security network for organisation
Download and install operation system updates on a regular basis will ensure window XP

network to avoid vulnerability and remove identified errors

A restrictive security policy while denying any traffic not specifically permitted

277.   Q: How does virus does in Computer?

A

There are programme deliberately created with my shows to spread the virus sent out by attackers. Virus hides by attaching itself to a file on the computer and is transferred to another computer through email file transfers and instant messages, it has potential to corrupt or giving files on your computer, use your email to spread itself to another computer, or even you raised your entire hardware drive

278.   Q; How does Stealth viruses work?

A

Stealth viruses can infect to computers and lay dormant until someone by the attacker.

279.   Q: How worm works inflicting computer?

A

A worm is and serve replicating program that is harmful to networks, uses the network to duplicate its code to the host on the network, often without any use intervention, it is different from viruses because a worm does not need to attached to a program worm problem is it consumes bandwidth which slowed down the network otherwise is total harmful.

280. Q; Describe how Trojan works?

A

A Trojan is technically a worm, does not need to be attached to other software. Instead Trojan threats is hidden in software that appears to do one thing and yet behind-the-scenes it does another.
The Trojan program can reproduce like a virus and spread to other computers, damage and production loss could be significant.

281. Q: Explain how Java works on computers

A

Java this is a program language that allows and nets applets to run within the were browser. Example of applets include a calculator or a counter.

Users from assessing normal services such as email and web server because the system is busy responding to abnormality large amounts of requestors works by sending enough request for a system resources that the requested service is overloaded and ceases to operate.

282. Q: What does DOS react on computer

A

 DOS attacks include ping of death this is a serial of repeated larger than normal that crash the receiving computer

283. Q; What does E mail bomb act dream?

A

E mail bomb this is large quantity of book email that overwhelmed the email server preventing from users from accessing it.

284. Q; How does DDOS act on computer

A.

Distributed denial of service(DDOS) is another form of attack that uses many infected computers called zombies, to lunch and attack, with the DDOS the intent is to

obstruct or overwhelm assets to the targeted
server, zombie computers located at
different geographical location make it
difficult to trace the origin of the attack.

285. Q: Describe how Span works on computer
      A
Span is used as a method of advertising,
however, can be used to send harmful links or
deceptive content. When used as an attack
method, spam may include links to an infected
website or and attachments, also lead you to
advertising sites. This windows are called pop-
ups

        Spam also known as junk mail.

286. Q How does social engineer behave?
A
 The social engineer Is a person who is able to
gain access to equipment or network by tricking
people into providing the necessary access
information..
Often the social engineer games the confidence
of an employee and convince the employee to
divulge username and password information

many antivirals and email software programs
automatically detect and remove spam from an
email inbox

287.   Q: Describe how computer is protecting

A

Protecting the computer

Here are some basic precaution to help protect
the computer.

Never give out your password.

Always acts for ID of unknown persons.

Restrict access of unexpected persons.

Escort all visitors.

Never post your password in your work.

Lock your computer when you leave your desk.

Do not let anyone follow you through a door that
requires an access card.

288.   Q: How can one guarantee that data on
   computer is saved?

A

The only way to fully ensure that data cannot be
recovered from a hard drive is to carefully shatter
the platers with a hammer and safely dispose of
the pieces.

When a computer is taking, the data is also stolen there are several metal of physically protecting computer equipment which include.

289. Q Name other ways to prevent the computer being physically being stolen.

A

Use cable lock with equipment.

Fit equipment with security screws.

Use security pages around equipment.

Label and install sensors, such as radio frequency identifier (RFID) tags

290. Q: How does Java scrip used to protect computer.

A

Control access to facilities Java script.

Programming language developed to enter without with HTML source code to allow interactive websites.

and keep telecommunication room locked.

291. Q: What other ways can you prevent computers hackers

Hackers may use any of these tools to install a program on a computer. To prevent against this attacks, most browsers have settings that forced the computer user to authorise the downloading or use of ActiveX, Java or Java script.

292. Q: What can be installed on computer by hackers without knowledge of the owner?

A

Adware, Spyware, and greyware are usually installed on a computer without the knowledge of this user. This program is correct information stored on the computer, change the computer configuration. Adware is a software program that displays advertising on your computer distributed with downloaded software.

293. Q: What is Malware

A

Malware is a file or program other than virus that is potentially harmful, many of attacks are phishing attacks that try to persuade the reader to knowingly provide attacker with access to personal information.

294. Q: What is Phishing

Phishing is a form of social engineering where the attacker pretends to represent a legitimate outside organisation such as a bank. A potential victim is contacted by email. The attacker might axe for verification of information such as a password or username

295. Q: What is the important of good Pass word

A.

Password protection, can prevent on authorised access to content, when assigning passwords the level of password control should much the level of protection required.

296. Q: What is the rules of password

Rules about password expiration and lock out should be defined. Look out rules apply where an unsuccessful attempt has been made to assess the system or when a specific change has been detected in the system configuration.

Password should expiry after a specific period of time. Password should contain a mixture of letters and numbers so that they cannot easily be broken.

297.   Q:How does (VPN) protect the computer data.

A

The Virtual private network (VPN) uses encryption to protect data, A VPN connection allows a remote user to safely assess resources as if their computer is physically attached to the local network.

Situations that require good security are usually deployed using a file system such as (NTFS

298. Q: Explain how WEP protect computer.

A

Wired equivalent privacy(WEP) the first generation security standard for wireless uses64-bit Parkers quickly discovered that64-bit WEP from encryption was easy to break, and attempts to overcome this weakness, most users employed a Wi-Fi protected access(WEP) which uses 128-bit or created by Cisco address the weakness in WEP &WPA.LEAP is a good choice when using Cisco equipment in conjunction with operating system like Windows and Linus wireless security techniques, disable the broad casting of the SSID to hide it from other users.

The security policy should identify hardware and equipment that can be used to prevent theft, vandalism, and data loss.

299. Q: What are some Physical security

Physical security involves four interrelated aspects which include access, data, in full structure and physical computer .

A

Restrict access to the premises with the following.

300. Q: What security recommend for
    hardware?

A

Fences.

Security hardware.

Protect the network infrastructure such as cabling, telecommunication equipment and network devices with the following.

301.   Q: What do one use to protect Secure
    tele-communication room.

    A

Wireless detector four on authorise access points.

Hardware firewalls.

Network management system that detects changes in using an patch panels.

302. Q: What is available to protect individual computer

A

Protect individual computer with the following

Cable lock the wall

 laptop docking station locks.

Lockable cases.

Lockable hard drive carriers.

Secure storage and transport of backup media

303. Q: What application to protect the hardware?

A

Security applications protect the operating system and software application data can be used to protect network devices.

Software firewall filters incoming data and is built into Windows and unusual network security.

304. Q: What can be used to protect operation system?

A

Application and OS patches.

Updates applications and the operating system to repair security weakness that are discovered

Logging and auditing.

Event logging and auditing should be enabled to monitor activities on the network.

The network administrator audits the log file of invent to investigate network access by on authorised users.

The intended recipients is only party to have the private key.

305. Q:Explain Asymmetric encryption

A.

Asymmetric encryption requires two keys and private and public key which can be widely distributed, including year mailing in clear text or posting on the web. But the private key is kept by an individual and must not be disclosed to any other party

306. Q: Explain Symmetric encryption

A

Symmetric encryption requires both side of an encrypted conversation to use on encryption key to encode and decode the data. The sender and receiver must both use identical keys symmetric encryption DES and DES are example

307. Q: What is Hash and according?

A

Hash and according the names of the most popular hashing algorithms are SHA and MD5

308. Q: What is VPN

A

VPN uses secure protocols to encryption and to secure data as if it was travelling in their privates tunnel. LAN even though the data actually over any network or Internet. The secure data pipelines between points in the VPN are called secure tunnels.

309. Q; Name few Physical security?

A

Physical security access control measures include

lot this is the most common device for
securing physical users.

Conduit is easing that protect the infra
structure media from damage.

Card key is a tool used to secure physical uses.
Video equipment's is records images and sound
for monitoring activities.
Security guard person controls access to the
entrance of the facility and monitoring activities
inside the facility

Two factors identification is a method to increase
security. Employees must use both password
and data security

310.   Q: what is Smart card.

A

Smart card is a device that has the ability to
store data safely. The internal memory is
embedded integrated circuit chips (ICC)
smartcards are used in many application word
wide such as ID badgers ,credit card payment..

Chapter 27

Author Qualification

1. BA (Hons), Law: include Criminal, Tort, damages, Contract, Property, Equity and Trust, European law, Public, Constitutional, Judicial Review, Agency.

2. (LLM)Master of Law; on legal research, and business, CSR Corporate social responsibility and human Right law" Institutional development and management, International Law.

3. Advance Dip. Business Law, Level 4: include Employment, Agency, Damages, Tort, Contract, employment tribunal etc.

4. Dip. Criminology

5. BA (Hons)op. Account: Financial Accountant and Management Accountant

6. Cert. Acct; Professional Certificate in Financial and Management Accounting

7. Dip. Book-keeping, Level 3

8. Nursing: RMN (Psychiatry trained nurse)

9. General Trained Nurse

10. Cert. in Education (Lecturer)

11. Business Certificate in Advanced

    Management

12. Cert. Business Enterprise

13. Advanced Food Hygiene

14. Intermediate Health and Safety

15. Dip. Safety Management

16. International Entrepreneur for over 25 years

17. Computers'. Cisco Level 2 Technician,

    (build, repair, networking)

18. Dip. Clait Plus (in all software)

19. New Clait Dip. Level 2

20. Microsoft Specialist

21. ECDL Level 2

22. Script writing: Dip. TV, radio, stage and film

23. Non-fiction writing: Dip. Autobiography,

    Biography and Family History

24. Cert. in Counselling

25. Author/Self-Publisher: Over 30 books

    published (2020)

26. Plumbing: Level 3 City and Guild

27. Theology: Cert. Bible studies; researched

    Theology for my PhD (most faiths)

28. Psychology and Social Science (university level certificate)

29. Photographer: Portrait, Glamour and Figure Photographer (PGFP).Dip.

30. Dip. Hypnotherapy

31. National Vocation Qualification (NVQ); Internal Verifier, (V1)

32. Trainer and Assessor A1 (NVQ)

33. RMA Registered Management award

Chapter 28

List of my published Books in 2019/20

In June 2019, I published the following books plus other books translated into Arabic, Spanish, French and Chinese, plus different formats such as eBooks,

Faith Books - in English Language

1. Love All Faiths

2. Faith Unity

3. Messengers

4. Islam v. Christianity

5. Allah Loves Islam

6. God Loves Christianity

7. God Enlighten Buddhism

8. Parama Nandra Loves Hindus

9. In Search of Wisdom in Freemasonry

10. Jesus Christ is Coming Soon

11. Psychology of Religion, Politics & Marriage

12 Jesus Christ, Prophets, Arch Angels and Saints over 150 poems

Non-Faith Books- in English Languages

1. The One - Over 130 Poems "DCF"

2. Mood Disorder

3. Sweet and Sour women (plus over 500 love letters from women)

4. The Law (Over 1,160 Questions and Answers)

5. Business law Volume 1

6. Business Law volume 2

7. set up and manage a business

8. How to set up a care home and care agency

9 How to manage a care Home and care agency

10. Care Home; Staff training

11. Criminology

12 over 150 Love Poems

13 over 100 poems on Faith and Victory

14over 100 poems on racism, discrimination and suffering

15 Psychology of religion, politics and marriage

16) Law and Religion

17.Financial Accounting

18. Management Accounting

19.Women are superior to men

The following are Translated completed and published books in June 2019.

The following translated in Spanish

1) Dios ama el Cristianismo (God loves Christianity)

2) V. Islamites Cristianismo (Islam v Christianity)

3)) De la Sabiduria En la Masoneri

(In search of Wisdom in freemasonry)

4) Ame todas Las creencias (love all faiths)

5) Mensageros De Dios (God's Messengers)

6)) Allah ama elIslam (allah loves Islam)

The following translated in French

1) Messagers de Dieu (god messengers)

2) Islamisme. v. Christianisme (Islam v Christianity)

3) A la recherche de la sagesse dans la franc-maçonnerie (In search of wisdom in freemasonry)

4) Aime Toutes les Fois (Love All faiths)

5) Dieu Aime Le Christianisme (God loves Christianity)

6) Allah aime l'Islam (Allah loves islam)

The following translated in Chines

上帝爱伊斯兰教 (Allah loves Islam)

伊斯蘭教訴基督教(Islam v Christianity)

The following translated in Arabic

الاسلام يحب الله. (Allah loves Islam)

الأديان جميع حب Love All Faiths

www.ingramcontent.com/pod-product-compliance
Lightning Source LLC
Chambersburg PA
CBHW051454030726
47592CB00006B/1918